THE
DEAL DESK
ADVANTAGE

THE
DEAL DESK
ADVANTAGE

Scale Faster. Close More Deals.
Turn Chaos into Revenue

JILL MARIE ROMAN

For more information, email info@dealsolutions.net.

ISBN: 979-8-89694-434-8 - Ebook

ISBN: 979-8-89694-435-5 - Paperback

ISBN: 979-8-89694-436-2 - Hardcover

CLAIM YOUR FREE DEAL DESK TOOLKIT!

To maximize your results from The Deal Desk Advantage, download my complementary resources at www.dealsolutions.net/forms. You'll get access to the Deal Desk Assessment Worksheet, Deal Desk Assessment Survey, and other valuable templates. Readers who use these practical tools implement their Deal Desk strategies up to 3x faster and quickly begin closing more profitable deals with greater efficiency. Don't just read about Deal Desk transformation—make it happen with these essential companion resources.

Deal Management Optimization Worksheet

B *I* U co X

Thank you for reading "The Deal Desk Advantage!"

Let's get you closer to closing more deals, scaling faster, and turning chaos into measurable revenue growth!

- Welcome to Your Deal Management Adventure

The Deal Desk Advantage Assessment Guide

B *I* U co X

This assessment evaluates your organization's deal management maturity across ten critical dimensions. Each dimension is scored on a scale of 1-5.

You can get a copy by visiting:

www.dealsolutions.net/forms

To my children, **Cassius and Carrera**, who shape my world in ways they may never fully know. Your growth, determination, and unique perspectives inspire me to evolve and excel in all that I do.

To every ambitious startup navigating the challenges of rapid growth—may these pages guide you in building stronger, more structured deal management strategies that help fuel your success.

And to the divine presence that guides my journey, I offer my deepest gratitude. Your light illuminates every step forward.

And so it is.

CONTENTS

Part 5: After Credits—The Human Element: Building a World-Class Deal Desk Culture

FOREWORD

December 31, 2018. The air in the office buzzed with tension, the kind of electric charge only felt at quarter-end. Forescout was in its first full fiscal year of reporting following its October 2017 IPO, and we were racing against the clock to finalize a deal that could make or break our Q4 numbers. The stakes? A $60 million government contract, winding its way through the labyrinth of federal procurement rules via a channel partner like Merlin International.

It was a classic end-of-year thriller. The deal was teetering on the brink, with critical stakeholders unavailable—some lost in the void of holiday vacations, others conveniently "out of pocket." The pricing structure on the order form no longer aligned with the customer's expectations. Adjustments were needed, but nothing short of precision and creativity would salvage this one.

Enter Jill Roman, our deal desk powerhouse, armed with spreadsheets that clarified even the most complex scenarios and a steady, pragmatic approach to navigating difficult salespeople. Jill wasn't just skilled at managing deals; she was a wizard at structuring deals to maximize profitability and contractual longevity. Her ability to structure pricing models, juggle competing priorities, and get interdepartmental approvals under pressure made her an invaluable part of the process.

That night, Jill and I found ourselves in a makeshift war room. I focused on revising the legal terms to align with government procurement standards, while Jill reworked the pricing structure to meet both the customer's demands and Forescout's financial objectives. It was a delicate balancing act, requiring ingenuity, collaboration, and more than a little caffeine.

By 11:59 p.m., the deal was signed. We had saved the quarter and contributed to a strong finish for Forescout. The company reported $84.7 million in revenue for Q4 2018, a 16% increase from Q4 2017. For the full year, revenues reached $297.7 million, reflecting a 35% year-over-year growth from 2017.[1] These numbers underscored Forescout's successful transition to life as a public company, bolstered by the relentless effort of teams like ours.

That night was just one example of what makes Jill Roman an extraordinary professional. After our time at Forescout, we teamed up again at SentinelOne, where we tackled even bigger deals and more ambitious goals, and were part of an even bigger IPO.

---

[1]   Motley Fool Transcribers, "ForeScout Technologies, Inc. (FSCT) Q4 2018 Earnings Conference Call Transcript," The Motley Fool, updated April 17, 2019, https://www.fool.com/earnings/call-transcripts/2019/02/07/forescout-technologies-inc-fsct-q4-2018-earnings-c.aspx.

SentinelOne's public offering on June 30, 2021, was a monumental success. It raised approximately $1.2 billion by offering 35 million shares at $35 per share, valuing the company at around $10 billion—a record-setting IPO for the cybersecurity industry.[2] As a leader in AI-driven endpoint protection, SentinelOne's rapid growth leading up to the IPO was extraordinary, with revenues doubling year-over-year to reach $93.1 million in fiscal year 2021.[3]

Jill played a critical role in this success, leading the deal desk team through a period of intense growth and high stakes. The team was responsible for structuring complex deals, securing interdepartmental alignment, and maintaining compliance with financial and legal standards. Under Jill's guidance, the deal desk optimized revenue-driving processes, streamlined approvals, and ensured that every transaction was aligned with SentinelOne's strategic goals. Her leadership helped establish the operational rigor and deal velocity needed to impress investors and deliver the kind of financial performance that fueled the IPO's success.

Across both companies, Jill consistently demonstrated professionalism, integrity, and an unshakable work ethic. She had an uncanny ability to navigate the most challenging

[2]   "SentinelOne Announces Pricing of Initial Public Offering," SentinelOne, June 30, 2021, https://www.sentinelone.com/press/sentinelone-announces-pricing-of-initial-public-offering/.

[3]   Robert Izquierdo, "Is This Cybersecurity IPO a Buy?" The Motley Fool, fool.com, August 3, 2021, https://www.fool.com/investing/2021/08/03/is-this-cybersecurity-ipo-stock-a-buy/#:~:text=The%20company%27s%202021%20fiscal%20year%2C%20which%20ended%20Jan.,%2437.4%20million%20from%20%2418%20million%20the%20year%20prior.

personalities and high-stakes situations, keeping the focus on outcomes while ensuring that every stakeholder felt heard and valued.

Now, Jill shares her expertise in *The Deal Desk Advantage*. This book is more than just a guide—it's a masterclass in building and optimizing deal processes. Jill's insights reflect her unique ability to bridge the worlds of sales, legal, and finance, providing readers with a clear roadmap for driving revenue growth and ensuring long-term success.

Jill, thank you for your friendship, your expertise, and for writing a book that captures the true power of the Deal Desk. To everyone reading this: you're about to unlock a transformative approach to deal management that will drive your business forward.

Best regards,

David Eric Thompson, Esq.

Attorney at Law

IT'S TIME TO STEP UP AND TAKE CONTROL!

Picture your business as a giant game of Jenga. Every decision you make is a block—one you're either carefully removing or strategically placing on top. In business, just like in Jenga, every move counts. Pull the wrong block, and everything could come crashing down, but with the right strategy and steady hands, you can build something extraordinary.

If you're running a startup, you know this balance all too well. Every deal could be the one that propels you to the next level—or the one that sends you back to square one. As your business scales, the complexity multiplies: bigger deals, higher stakes, and more moving parts. And yet, like many growing companies, you might still be winging it without a dedicated system or team in place. That's not just risky; it's a recipe for missed opportunities, compliance nightmares, and stunted growth potential.

WHY YOUR STARTUP NEEDS A DEAL DESK

A Deal Desk isn't just another corporate buzzword—it's your startup's secret weapon for sustainable growth. Think of it as your command center: where strategy meets execution. It's the place where complex deals are structured, pricing is optimized, and compliance is guaranteed. But more importantly, it's where the future of your company's success is secured—deal by deal.

I've seen firsthand what a Deal Desk can do. Companies I've worked with have increased deal velocity by 40 percent and boosted average deal sizes by 33 percent in just one year. One startup I helped grew its revenue by a staggering 101 percent over three years, all while maintaining tight control over margins and compliance. These aren't just numbers—they're transformations that can determine whether a startup scales or stalls.

MY JOURNEY TO THE DEAL DESK

Sometimes, the best lessons come from unexpected places. I can attest as my unconventional path eventually led me to discover my passion for deal management.

Fresh out of college with a psychology degree, I found myself at a crossroads. What started as a temporary role as a nanny for an NFL player's family turned into an eight-and-a-half-year adventure that taught me invaluable lessons about adaptability, resilience, and seizing opportunities as they came. Little did I know, these skills would become the foundation of my career.

Fast forward to my time at Adobe, where I faced another pivotal moment when my department was being relocated, and my career path felt uncertain. Moving to another state was the requirement for a managerial promotion, but around that time, my VP approached me with a new opportunity: a role in the Deal Desk. He believed I had the skills to thrive in this position, and after some thought, I decided to take the leap. That decision changed everything.

I fully immersed myself in the world of deal management, where I discovered a passion I didn't know existed. The role allowed me to transition from simply accounting for agreements and revenue after execution to actively shaping agreements, negotiating pricing and business terms, and developing complex deal strategies. It was exhilarating and rewarding—evidenced by the seven deal-related awards I received during my time in this role.

Over the years, my career spanned roles in legal, finance, revenue auditing, and accounting, giving me a holistic perspective on deal processes. My expertise grew further during my 11 years dedicated exclusively to Deal Desks. I've had the privilege of working with major corporations like Adobe and Oracle, where I learned the critical importance of compliance and robust deal strategies. Later, I applied these lessons to high-growth startups, turning struggling ventures into deal-closing powerhouses.

This blend of big-company rigor and startup agility has been the hallmark of my career. It's given me the unique ability to craft comprehensive playbooks, build flexible approval matrices, and forge crucial stakeholder relationships that drive success. Every role, every pivot, and every leap prepared me for this—it's why I'm so passionate about helping startups unlock their full potential through Deal Desks.

WHAT THIS BOOK WILL TEACH YOU

This book is your ultimate guide to building a Deal Desk that's not just functional but transformative. By the time you've turned the last page, you'll have learned how to:

- Build a scalable Deal Desk tailored to your startup

- Create comprehensive playbooks and approval matrices that streamline operations

- Forge crucial stakeholder relationships to drive alignment

- Accelerate deal velocity while safeguarding compliance

- Structure deals for maximum profitability

- Prepare your company for public scrutiny and investor confidence

THE COST OF WAITING

In today's fast-paced market, waiting is the enemy of progress. Lack of deal oversight isn't just inefficient—it's dangerous. Compliance issues and financial missteps can sink your startup faster than you can say "IPO." The market has zero tolerance for errors, and a robust Deal Desk is your best defense.

Remember our Jenga metaphor? The higher your tower grows, the more crucial every move becomes. But with a well-structured Deal Desk, you'll have steady hands and a clear vision to keep building. You'll know which blocks to pull, when to pull them, and how to transform calculated risks into strategic advantages.

YOUR NEXT MOVE

This book is your blueprint for building a world-class Deal Desk, explicitly tailored to your startup's needs. Whether you're starting from scratch or refining an existing process, you'll find the tools, strategies, and insights you need to turn your deal process into your competitive edge.

It's time to stop wingin' it. Your startup's next chapter begins now. Let's turn your deal management into the secret weapon that fuels explosive growth. The spotlight is on you; it's time to take center stage. Action!

While this book provides a comprehensive guide to building and optimizing your Deal Desk, some organizations may benefit from expert assistance. **Deal Solutions** *offers tailored services to support businesses at every stage of their Deal Desk journey, from initial setup to ongoing optimization.*

PART 1

THE DEAL DESK IMPERATIVE

CHAPTER 1

THE GROWTH CHALLENGE

Imagine standing at the edge of possibility, blueprints in hand, ready to build not just a business, but a legacy. That's where every entrepreneur starts—with a vision of what could be. But here's the truth that nobody tells you: **the distance between vision and reality isn't measured in steps; it's measured in transformations.**

My path to understanding transformational growth started in retail, of all places. What began as a part-time job at Contempo Casuals turned into my first lesson in rapid scaling and adaptation. Within just a couple of months, I was promoted to Assistant Manager and, shortly after that, to Co-Manager. Little did I know, this early experience in managing operations and people would lay the groundwork for my future career.

That was just the beginning of what I like to call my "triple-life symphony." By day, I was navigating the intricate world of bankruptcy law from the fifteenth floor of the Pruneyard

Towers in Campbell, California, where every case was a master class in negotiation and human psychology. Picture this: A small office filled with towering stacks of case files, each one representing a person or business at their most vulnerable moment. My desk was central command for orchestrating complex negotiations between creditors who wanted their money and clients who were fighting to keep their dreams alive.

Here's where I learned one of the most valuable lessons about deal-making: sometimes, the most powerful position is understanding where everybody's problems lie. I spent hours on the phone with creditors, learning to read between the lines of their demands, finding those small openings where compromise could bloom. One moment, I was negotiating with a major bank's legal team over a business restructuring; the next, I was working with a family trying to keep their home. Each conversation was a delicate dance of empathy and strategy.

But the real gold mine of experience? Contract analysis. Every day, I'd dive deep into agreements that could either save or sink our clients. We were discussing dissecting every clause, condition, and carefully worded promise. I learned to spot the hidden landmines in seemingly innocent language—the kind of skill that would prove invaluable in future deal negotiations. Working alongside the bankruptcy trustee taught me that every detail matters when you're building something meant to last.

When I reflect on my time there, one case in particular stands out. We had a small business owner—let's call him Mike—who'd built a promising manufacturing company but got caught in a perfect storm of market changes and a few bad deals. As I pored over his contracts, I discovered a pattern of seemingly small compromises that had snowballed into significant vulnerabilities. It was like watching a slow-motion replay of how not to structure business agreements. That experience burned into my mind the importance of having robust systems for managing complex deals—a lesson that would later become the foundation of my Deal Desk philosophy.

The bankruptcy court was my first real glimpse into how businesses rise and fall based on their ability to structure and manage agreements. I watched companies that looked unstoppable on paper crumble because they didn't have the right systems in place to manage their growth. But I also saw businesses rise from the ashes because they learned from their mistakes and built better foundations.

As the sun set, part two of the "triple-life symphony" began. I transformed into something entirely unexpected—a 5'4", 120-pound bouncer at the Cactus Club in downtown San Jose.

Now, you might be wondering: how does someone barely taller than a filing cabinet convince people that they're a security threat? Here's where I learned my first lesson about the power of perception: my partner Stikmon and I crafted a story about my supposed karate expertise. And you know what? It worked.

People believed what we presented with conviction—a lesson that would serve me well in the deal-making world years later.

But wait, there's more. Add "bartender extraordinaire" to the mix, and you've got someone who's unknowingly preparing for a future in deal orchestration. Think about it—a legal assistant by day, measuring every word in contracts; a bouncer by night, reading people and defusing situations; and a bartender in between, mixing just the right ingredients for success. The universe was preparing me for something bigger, even if I couldn't see it yet.

Then, like many caught in the intoxicating spirit of entrepreneurship, I took a leap into the unknown. With my then-boyfriend, now-husband and a group of dreamers, we launched Ultravibe.com (note the URL is no longer owned by us)—a platform showcasing unsigned musical talent through live-streamed performances. Sound familiar? We were basically trying to build YouTube before YouTube existed, with a focus on live music.

The *Mercury News* even caught wind of our vision, plastering our launch party at The Edge across their cover with the headline "Rock It Launch." We were riding high, traveling up and down California, capturing raw talent and pure energy. We were building our own skyscraper, but here's the catch—we were doing it without a blueprint.

After about three years, our tower of dreams had crumbled, becoming another statistic of the dot-com burst. But here's where the magic of perspective comes in: what seemed like failure was actually the universe's way of preparing me for my true calling.

Every role I played—the detail-oriented legal assistant, the people-reading bouncer, the solution-mixing bartender, and the visionary startup founder—was a piece of the puzzle that would eventually create a Deal Desk expert. Each experience taught me something crucial about what businesses need to survive and thrive.

It isn't just Mike's story that cemented the importance of deals. Let me share another story that brings this all home. Meet Olivia, creator of HydroSmarte, an innovative water bottle company born in her garage. Like many entrepreneurs, she started with pure passion and a clear vision: one person, one product, one dream. But success has a way of creating its own challenges.

As HydroSmarte grew from a garage project into a nationwide phenomenon, Olivia found herself playing a high-stakes game of Jenga with her business. Each new deal, each new opportunity, was another block added to an increasingly unstable tower. She was doing what many of us do—trying to build a skyscraper without a blueprint, managing million-dollar deals with the same systems she used when selling to neighbors.

Sound familiar? It should. Whether you're streaming underground music or selling smart water bottles, the growth challenge remains the same: how do you scale your vision without losing your soul? How do you manage increasing complexity without sacrificing the passion that started it all?

This is where the Deal Desk comes in—not just as a department or a process, but as a transformation catalyst. Think of it as your business's control tower, orchestrating every deal with surgical precision, diplomatic finesse, perfect balance, and entrepreneurial vision.

The truth is that every entrepreneur faces their moment of reckoning—that point where passion meets process, where vision meets reality. For Olivia, it was drowning in paperwork while her innovation gathered dust. For me, it was watching Ultravibe dissolve, knowing we had the right idea but the wrong execution.

But here's the beautiful thing about entrepreneurship: every "failure" is just preparation for your next breakthrough. My journey from bouncer to Deal Desk expert wasn't a straight line—it was a transformation. And that's exactly what your business needs to go through to reach its next level.

As we dive deeper into the world of Deal Desks, remember this: You're not just building a system; you're creating a transformation machine. One that will turn chaos into clarity, potential into performance, and dreams into reality.

Are you ready to build your skyscraper? This time, with a blueprint in hand?

Let's begin.

CHAPTER 2

INTRODUCING THE DEAL DESK

YOUR OASIS IN THE DESERT OF DEAL MANAGEMENT

As we dive into the concept of Deal Desks, it's important to understand that the skills required for effective deal management often have unexpected origins. In my case, the foundation of my deal-making prowess was laid long before I ever set foot in a boardroom. You see, my first taste of the business world came much earlier than you might expect… all the way back to a childhood summer, when I became an entrepreneur at the ripe old age of eight. That's right, folks—while most kids were dreaming of ice cream trucks and cartoon marathons, I was busy learning the ropes of the cutthroat world of...pea picking!

It was dark, it was early, and my sister and I were being dropped off at a farm by our mom. Our trusty bikes? Our getaway vehicles. Our mission? Pick as many peas as humanly possible before the sun graces us with its presence. I still can't tell you why my older brother wasn't included in this fun summer activity.

This wasn't your average summer gig. We were paid by the bushel, and while I can't remember the exact rate, I do remember thinking I'd need to pick approximately a zillion peas to afford that Barbie dream house.

But here's the kicker—this wasn't just about making money. Oh no, this was boot camp for life skills. Determination? Check. Work ethic? Double check. The ability to differentiate between a pea and a bug while half asleep? Triple check!

After hours of channeling our inner pea-picking machines, we'd hop on our bikes and pedal home. Remember, this was the era of latchkey kids (where kids came home after school to an empty house while both parents worked) and limited parental supervision—no cell phones, no GPS, just pure kid power and a whole lot of leg muscle.

The best part of the day? Crawling into my Barbie sleeping bag, feeling like I'd just conquered Mount Everest. It was a bit like that scene in the movie Napoleon Dynamite where they're milking cows—except, thankfully, our challenge was small, green, round, and didn't moo.

You might be thinking, "Jill, that sounds awful!" But those grueling summers in the pea fields laid the foundation for everything I've accomplished since. They taught me that success isn't about waiting for opportunities to fall into your lap—it's about getting up before dawn, putting in the work, and not stopping until you've filled your bushel.

So, the next time you're facing a challenge that seems as endless as a field of peas, remember this: if an eight-year-old can spend her summer picking peas and still come out smiling, you can handle whatever life throws at you. And who knows? Maybe those challenges are just preparing you for your next big business breakthrough.

You might be wondering what picking peas has to do with Deal Desks. Well, as it turns out, everything. Those early mornings in the pea fields taught me invaluable lessons about hard work, persistence, and the importance of systems and processes—all crucial elements in effective deal management.

As I had learned to navigate those endless rows of peas efficiently, a well-structured Deal Desk helps businesses navigate complex transactions. And believe me, negotiating million-dollar deals can sometimes feel just as challenging as distinguishing between a pea and a giant hornworm before the crack of dawn!

So, as we explore the intricacies of Deal Desks and their transformative power in business, remember: every great journey starts somewhere. Mine started in a pea field. Where did yours begin? How will you leverage your path to transform your journey?

With that context in mind, let's explore what exactly a Deal Desk is and how it embodies the same principles of efficiency, perseverance, and a systematic approach that I learned in those pea fields.

Imagine you are lost in a vast, scorching desert. The sun beats down mercilessly, and an endless sea of sand stretches out before you in every direction. Your throat is parched, your energy levels are plummeting, and you feel like you're trudging through quicksand with every step. When you think all hope is lost, you spot an oasis on the horizon—a lush, green paradise, complete with swaying palm trees and a crystal-clear pool of water.

In the world of business, that desert is the landscape of deal management—a harsh, unforgiving environment where even the most seasoned professionals can quickly find themselves lost and overwhelmed. And that oasis? That's the Deal Desk—a haven of structure, support, and refreshment amid the chaos.

DEAL DESK 101

At its core, a Deal Desk is a centralized hub for all things deal-related. It's a specialized team composed of professionals with diverse backgrounds in areas such as sales, legal, finance, and/or operations who work together to streamline the deal process, ensure consistency, and drive revenue growth. Think of it as a command center for your deals, where all the moving parts come together as a well-oiled deal machine.

No matter what anybody tells you, words
and ideas can change the world.

—*Dead Poets Society*

But a Deal Desk is more than just a team or a set of processes—
it's a philosophy, a way of thinking about deals that puts clarity,
collaboration, and customer success at the forefront. It's about
breaking down silos, fostering communication, and ensuring
that everyone is working toward the same goal: closing deals
that benefit both the company and the customer.

The Anatomy of a Deal Desk

So, what exactly makes up a Deal Desk? While every
organization's Deal Desk may look a little different, a few key
components are essential to success:

1. **People:** Professionals are the heart of any Deal Desk;
   the ones who make it run. These individuals can
   come from a diverse array of backgrounds, including
   but not limited to sales, sales operations, accounting,
   legal, pricing, finance, and revenue management. This
   cross-functional team works in concert to keep deals
   moving smoothly. The beauty of a Deal Desk lies in
   this diversity of expertise; each team member brings
   their unique skills, experiences, and perspectives
   to the table, creating a cohesive, high-performing
   unit. This blend of talents allows the Deal Desk to
   address complex deal scenarios from multiple angles,
   ensuring thorough analysis and optimal outcomes.

The collective knowledge and collaborative spirit of these professionals form the lifeblood of an effective Deal Desk, driving its success and impact on the organization.

2. **Processes**: A Deal Desk is only as good as the processes that guide it. From deal qualification to pricing approvals to contract reviews, a Deal Desk must have clearly defined workflows and standard operating procedures in place to ensure consistency and efficiency. These processes are the guardrails that keep deals on track and prevent them from veering off into the proverbial desert.

3. **Technology**: In today's fast-paced business environment, technology is the fuel that keeps the Deal Desk engine running. From Customer Relationship Management (CRM) systems to Configure, Price, and Quote (CPQ) software to contract management tools, a Deal Desk must be equipped with the right tech stack to automate manual tasks, provide real-time data and insights, and enable seamless collaboration across teams.

4. **Metrics**: You can't manage what you don't measure, and that's especially true when it comes to deals. A Deal Desk must have a robust set of metrics and key performance indicators (KPIs) in place to track the health of deals, identify constraints and inefficiencies, and measure the impact of the Deal Desk on revenue growth. These metrics are the signposts that guide the

Deal Desk on its journey, helping it stay on course and make data-driven decisions.

The Benefits of a Deal Desk

As the picture of a Deal Desk comes into focus, we can visualize and discuss the benefits. What can a Deal Desk actually do for your organization? As it turns out, quite a lot.

1. **Faster deal velocity**: By streamlining processes and automating manual tasks, a Deal Desk can significantly reduce the time it takes to move a deal from start to finish. This means more deals closed in less time, and more revenue hitting your bottom line.

2. **Improved deal quality**: A Deal Desk ensures every deal meets a consistent set of standards and criteria, from pricing to legal terms to product fit. This leads to higher-quality deals that are more likely to close and maintain long-term value.

3. **Better collaboration**: A Deal Desk breaks down the barriers between teams, fostering a culture of collaboration and communication. This leads to a more cohesive, aligned organization that can move faster and adapt to change more easily.

4. **Increased efficiency**: By centralizing deal management and eliminating redundant processes, a Deal Desk can dramatically increase operational efficiency. This frees up time and resources that can

instead be spent on high-value activities like selling and innovating.

5. **Stronger customer relationships**: A Deal Desk puts the customer at the center of the deal process, ensuring that their needs and expectations are met every step of the way. This leads to happier, more satisfied customers who are more likely to stick around for the long haul.

The Deal Desk in Action

To really understand the power of a Deal Desk, let's look at a hypothetical scenario. Meet AcmeCorp, a fast-growing software company that was struggling to keep up with the demands of its expanding customer base. Deals were taking months—sometimes years—to close, and there was little consistency in pricing, terms, or product offerings.

Enter the AcmeCorp Deal Desk. Led by an elite team of deal management experts, the Deal Desk quickly got to work streamlining processes, implementing new technologies, and establishing a set of metrics to track progress. They worked with sales to create a standardized deal qualification process, collaborated with legal to develop a library of pre-approved contract clauses, and partnered with finance to build a dynamic pricing model that could adapt to changing market conditions.

The results were nothing short of remarkable. Within just a few months, AcmeCorp saw a 50 percent reduction in deal cycle times, a 20 percent increase in average deal size, and a 30 percent improvement in customer satisfaction scores. The Deal Desk transformed AcmeCorp's deal management process from a liability into a competitive advantage, setting the stage for continued growth and success.

NAVIGATING THE DEAL DESK JOURNEY

Building a Deal Desk is not a one-size-fits-all proposition. Every organization's journey will differ based on factors like company size, industry, sales model, and organizational culture. But regardless of your specific situation, you can take a few key steps to set yourself up for Deal Desk success:

1. **Assess your current state**: Before you can chart a course for your Deal Desk journey, you need to understand where you're starting from. Take a hard look at your current deal management process and identify challenge areas and areas for improvement.

2. **Define your goals**: What do you want your Deal Desk to achieve? Faster deal velocity? Better collaboration? Increased efficiency? Clearly defining your goals upfront will help you build a Deal Desk that's tailored to your specific needs and objectives.

3. **Secure executive buy-in**: A Deal Desk is a significant undertaking that requires support from the highest levels of the organization. Ensure you have your executive team's backing before you embark on your Deal Desk journey.

4. **Start small and evolve**: Rome wasn't built in a day, and neither is a Deal Desk. Start with a small, focused pilot program, and use lessons learned from the pilot to expand and refine your Deal Desk gradually over time.

5. **Celebrate your successes**: Building a Deal Desk is hard work, and taking time to recognize and celebrate your achievements along the way is important. Share your wins with the rest of the organization and use them to build momentum and support for your ongoing Deal Desk efforts.

The Future of Deal Management

As we look to the future of deal management, one thing is clear: the Deal Desk is here to stay. As businesses become more complex, global, and data-driven, the need for a centralized, streamlined approach to deal management will only continue to grow.

Today's Deal Desks are already leveraging artificial intelligence (AI) to enhance their capabilities. AI-powered tools are being used to automate repetitive tasks, analyze vast amounts of data for insights, and provide predictive analytics. For instance, some Deal Desks are using AI to:

1. Predict deal outcomes based on historical data and current market conditions

2. Optimize pricing strategies in real-time

3. Automate parts of the contract generation process

4. Identify potential risks or red flags in deal structures

However, this is just the beginning. As AI technologies continue to evolve and mature, the Deal Desk of tomorrow will be even more powerful and strategic. We're moving toward a world where AI can:

1. Autonomously negotiate deal terms within predefined parameters

2. Generate fully customized contracts based on a customer's specific needs and preferences

3. Provide real-time coaching to sales reps during customer interactions

4. Predict market trends and suggest proactive deal strategies

These advancements will transform the role of the Deal Desk from tactical support to strategic driver of business growth and success. Deal Desk professionals will increasingly focus on high-level strategy, relationship management, and complex problem-solving, while AI handles more of the day-to-day operational tasks.

As organizations continue to experiment with and adopt these cutting-edge technologies, the boundaries of what's possible in deal management are constantly expanding. The future Deal Desk will be a powerful blend of human expertise and AI capabilities, driving unprecedented levels of efficiency, effectiveness, and strategic value for businesses of all sizes.

CONCLUSION

Crossing the desert of deal management can be daunting, as it is full of hidden pitfalls and treacherous terrain. But with a Deal Desk, you have the tools, expertise, and support you need to navigate this landscape with confidence and success.

So, if you're feeling lost in the desert of deals, don't despair. Look to the horizon, where the oasis of the Deal Desk awaits. Take a deep breath, take a step forward, and begin your journey toward a new era of deal management excellence.

Whether you're navigating a field of peas or a complex business deal, the principles remain the same: start early, work systematically, and don't stop until you've filled your bushel—or in this case, closed your deal. Much like my childhood summer job, a Deal Desk provides structure, encourages persistence, and ultimately leads to sweet success—though I must say, the rewards in business are usually much more substantial than a few dollars per bushel!

And remember: with a Deal Desk set up, the possibilities are endless. You've got this.

CHAPTER 3

THE DEAL DESK DIFFERENCE

ORCHESTRATING GROWTH, ONE DEAL AT A TIME

From Chaos to Concerto

Imagine a bustling orchestra, each instrument as a department—sales, legal, revenue, finance. In the early days, the music was raw and passionate but disorganized. Sales threw out leads, legal scrambled with contracts, and finance juggled numbers in a disconnected frenzy. The potential for a symphony exists, but without a conductor, it's just noise.

Enter the Deal Desk: Your Maestro

This is where the Deal Desk steps in, transforming your business from a cacophony into a well-rehearsed concerto. It's your maestro, guiding each department, ensuring everyone plays their part at the right time, with perfect harmony. Let's explore how a Deal Desk orchestrates growth and unlocks the full potential of your deals.

> *No one can whistle a symphony. It takes*
> *a whole orchestra to play it.*
>
> — *H.E. Luccock*

In the fast-paced world of business, it's easy to get caught up in the day-to-day grind of closing deals and chasing revenue. But what if you could not only survive but also thrive in this high-pressure environment? What if you could transform your deal management process from a source of stress and frustration into a well-oiled machine that consistently delivers results?

A Deal Desk is your secret weapon in the battle for business success. But what exactly makes a Deal Desk so powerful? What sets it apart from other approaches to deal management? Let's explore the unique benefits of a Deal Desk and discover how it can help you take your business to the next level.

BENEFIT #1: STREAMLINED PROCESSES

A Deal Desk creates a centralized hub that eliminates bottlenecks and accelerates deal flow.

- Creates a standardized playbook for all deal-related activities, ensuring consistency and efficiency

- Acts as the connective tissue between departments, minimizing miscommunications

- Coordinates inputs from sales, legal, revenue, finance, and operations in a structured manner

- Reduces wasted time and effort by breaking down departmental silos

- Transforms the disjointed back-and-forth between departments into a synchronized workflow

- Allows each department to leverage its expertise effectively in the deal process

- Results in a more cohesive, efficient deal workflow with clear, unified direction

BENEFIT #2: IMPROVED DEAL QUALITY

A Deal Desk ensures you're not just closing deals, but closing the right deals that drive sustainable growth.

- Applies rigorous vetting to ensure deals meet company standards for profitability, risk, and strategic fit

- Makes pricing strategy a precision instrument, finely tuned to maximize revenue without sacrificing competitiveness

- Eliminates guesswork through data-driven analysis and market intelligence

- Ensures every quote hits the sweet spot, capturing full value while remaining attractive to customers

- Prevents revenue leakage by optimally positioning your products against competitors

- Reviews legal terms to minimize exposure and protect your interests

- Assesses product fit to ensure you're delivering real value to customers

- Builds a portfolio of high-quality deals that drive sustainable, profitable growth

BENEFIT #3: ENHANCED COLLABORATION

A Deal Desk breaks down silos and fosters cross-functional teamwork that unlocks innovation.

- Creates a shared space for communication and collaboration across departments

- Tears down walls that typically separate different functional areas

- Taps into specialized expertise from legal, finance, and operations at the right time

- Brings diverse perspectives together to solve problems and seize opportunities

- Creates an environment where creative collaboration can thrive

- Encourages the collision of ideas that spark innovation

- Unlocks the full potential of your organization through collective intelligence

- Builds stronger interdepartmental relationships and mutual understanding

BENEFIT #4: DATA-DRIVEN INSIGHTS

A Deal Desk transforms raw deal data into actionable intelligence that drives continuous improvement.

- Provides a centralized repository for all deal-related data

- Offers unprecedented visibility into deal health and performance

- Identifies patterns and trends by analyzing metrics like cycle times, win rates, and average deal sizes

- Pinpoints constraints in your process that might otherwise go unnoticed

- Highlights top-performing representatives and strategies

- Guides data-driven decisions about resource allocation

- Enables targeted actions to address specific issues in your deal process

- Eliminates guesswork with a clear, data-driven path to success

BENEFIT #5: SCALABILITY AND AGILITY

A Deal Desk creates a flexible framework that grows with your business and adapts to changing market conditions.

- Scales to handle increasing deal volume as your business expands

- Adapts to new markets, geographies, products, or pricing models

- Forms specialized teams to handle unique requirements of different markets

- Rapidly develops and tests new pricing strategies without disrupting existing business

- Creates custom deal structures and approval workflows as needed

- Provides training and support for new offerings or processes

- Offers a solid foundation for growth while maintaining flexibility

- Functions like a well-designed house that can be reconfigured as your needs evolve

PUTTING IT ALL TOGETHER

The true power of a Deal Desk lies in how these benefits work together to create a whole greater than the sum of its parts.

- Streamlined processes + improved deal quality = a deal management machine that consistently delivers high-value, low-risk deals
- Enhanced collaboration + data-driven insights = a culture of continuous improvement and innovation
- All elements + scalable framework = a business built for long-term success and growth

The Acme Odyssey: A Deal Desk Transformation Tale

Setting the Stage

Once upon a time, at the bustling enterprise of Acme Corporation, the deal process was as wild as the Wild West. The sales team slung deals like cowboys at a rodeo, but often, their lassos missed the mark, snagging on legal and finance hurdles.

The Transformation Begins

Enter the Deal Desk—Acme's new sheriff in town. This wasn't just any sheriff; it was an expert strategist, a diplomatic genius, who could align every department under a single banner. Led by the legendary Fiona, a maestro of deal orchestration, the Deal Desk was about to turn the chaos into a masterpiece.

Act I: Streamlining Processes

Fiona introduced the 'Deal Dance,' a choreographed routine that had every department moving in harmony. Where once deals stumbled through approvals like clumsy ballerinas, they now glided gracefully from sales to finance to legal, each step perfectly timed to a Tchaikovsky suite.

Act II: Raising the Bar on Deal Quality

Fiona, with a chef's discerning palate, ensured no deal reached the table unless it was Michelin-star worthy. Under her guidance, Acme's deals became gourmet offerings—scrumptiously crafted and beautifully plated to impress even the most discerning of clients.

Act III: Fostering Innovation

In Fiona's workshop, innovation was the currency. She equipped her team with the tools to innovate—from AI analytics to collaborative platforms—turning the Deal Desk into an inventor's paradise, where every challenge was met with a groundbreaking solution.

Curtain Call: A Cultural Symphony

Finally, Fiona wove a tapestry of culture so tightly knit that every thread—each department—pulled together to create a vibrant, dynamic pattern. Acme's Deal Desk didn't just function: it thrived, driven by a shared mission to excel.

Epilogue: The Results

By the time the curtain fell on Fiona's first year, the Deal Desk had cut deal cycle times in half, revenues per deal soared, and employee satisfaction hit the high notes. Acme

Corporation had not just a functional Deal Desk but a strategic powerhouse, cited by the CEO in every shareholder meeting as the cornerstone of Acme's market success.

As we end our tale of Acme's transformation, think about your own Deal Desk. Imagine the legends that could be told of its triumphs and the victories yet to come. Like Fiona and her team, you have the power to script your own saga of success. So, take the reins, and let your Deal Desk team be the hero of your corporate story.

CONCLUSION

The world of business is a wild and unpredictable place. Deals can make or break a company, and the stakes are always high. But with a Deal Desk, you have a powerful ally that can help you navigate even the roughest waters.

A Deal Desk can be the difference between just surviving and truly thriving by streamlining your processes, improving your deal quality, enhancing your collaboration, harnessing your data, and scaling with your business. It can help you close more deals faster, with less risk, and with more reward. It can help you build a culture of excellence and innovation that can withstand the test of time.

So, if you're ready to take your deal management game to the next level, transform your business, and achieve new heights of success, then it's time to invest in a Deal Desk. With a Deal Desk, the possibilities are endless, and the future is bright.

PART 2

BUILDING YOUR DREAM DEAL DESK

CHAPTER 4

ASSESSING YOUR NEEDS

You've heard the buzz about Deal Desks and how they can revolutionize your business. You're excited about the possibilities and eager to get started. But hold on just a moment—before you dive headfirst into building your Deal Desk, you need to take a step back and assess what your business needs.

Think of it like planning for a road trip. You wouldn't just jump in the car and start driving without first figuring out where you're going, how you're going to get there, and what you'll need along the way. The same principle applies to building a Deal Desk. If you don't take the time to assess your needs upfront, you risk ending up with a Deal Desk that doesn't fit your business, your customers, or your goals.

THE IMPORTANCE OF A NEEDS ASSESSMENT

The first critical step in building your Deal Desk is understanding your current landscape. By thoroughly examining your deal management process, you'll uncover sticking points, recognize untapped potential, and establish clear objectives for your future Deal Desk framework.

Why is an assessment so critical? For starters, it helps ensure that your Deal Desk is tailored to your unique business needs. Every organization is different, with its own culture, processes, and challenges. What works for one company may not work for another. By assessing your specific needs, you can build a Deal Desk that is customized to your business and designed to solve your most pressing problems.

The needs assessment also helps you avoid costly mistakes and rework down the road. If you build your Deal Desk based on assumptions or best guesses, you may find that it doesn't actually meet your needs or solve your problems. You may have to go back to the drawing board, wasting valuable time and resources in the process. By doing your due diligence upfront, you can avoid these pitfalls and set yourself up for success.

THE NEEDS ASSESSMENT PROCESS

So, how do you go about assessing your needs? The process can be broken down into three key steps:

Step 1: Map Your Current Process

The first step in needs assessment is to map out your current deal management process from start to finish. This means documenting every step from lead generation to deal closure and everything in between.

As you map out your process, pay close attention to the following:

- Who is involved in each step of the process? What are their roles and responsibilities?

- What tools and systems do you currently use to manage deals? How well do they work?

- What data do you collect and track throughout the process? How is this data used to inform decision-making?

- How long does each step of the process typically take? Where are the impediments and delays?

The goal of process mapping is to create a clear, comprehensive picture of how your current deal management process works. This will serve as a baseline against which you can identify areas for improvement and define your future state. There are several different programs that you can use to help with mapping, e.g., Miro, Lucidchart, Asana, SmartDraw, and Planio, to name a few.

Step 2: Identify Obstacles and Opportunities

Once you have a clear map of your current process, the next step is to identify your obstacles and opportunities. This is where you'll start to uncover the specific problems you want your Deal Desk to solve and the benefits you hope to achieve.

Understanding your organization's specific needs is the first step towards creating an effective Deal Desk. This involves identifying frustrations, chokepoints, and opportunities for improvement.

Failure is not an option.

—Apollo 13

As you identify your problem areas, don't just focus on the symptoms—dig deeper to uncover the root causes. For example, if you're experiencing long deal cycles, is it because of inefficient processes, lack of standardization, or poor team communication? The more specific you can be about the underlying issues, the better equipped you'll be to design a Deal Desk that addresses them.

Take a moment to reflect: What are the biggest hurdles in your current deal process? Write them down. Now, imagine a world where these sticking points are resolved. How does that change your workflow? Your mindset?

In addition to obstacles, you should also look for opportunities to improve and optimize your deal management process. These might include:

- Automating manual tasks to free up time for high-value work

- Leveraging data and analytics to make informed decisions

- Standardizing and streamlining processes to reduce errors and inconsistencies

- Enhancing collaboration and communication between teams

- Improving the customer experience throughout the deal process

By identifying both your challenges and opportunities, you'll get a sense of what your ideal future state looks like and what your Deal Desk needs to achieve.

Step 3: Define Your Goals and Requirements

The ultimate step in needs assessment is to define your goals and requirements for your Deal Desk. To do this, take everything you've learned from process mapping and pain point identification and translate it into a clear, actionable plan.

Your goals should be specific, measurable, achievable, relevant, and time-bound (SMART). Some examples of Deal Desk goals might include:

- Reducing average deal cycle time by 25 percent within the next six months

- Improving win rates by 15 percent over the next year

- Increasing average deal size by 10 percent within the next quarter

- Reducing the number of manual touchpoints in the deal process by 50 percent within the next three months

In addition to defining your goals, you should also define the requirements for your Deal Desk. These are the specific capabilities, features, and functionalities that your Deal Desk needs to meet your goals and solve your problems. Some examples of Deal Desk requirements might include:

- Automated pricing and quoting tools

- Centralized contract management and approval workflows

- Real-time pipeline visibility and reporting

- Collaborative deal rooms for cross-functional teams

- Integration with existing Customer Relationship Management (CRM) and Enterprise Resource Planning (ERP) systems

By clearly defining your goals and requirements upfront, you'll create a roadmap for your Deal Desk that ensures it meets your needs and delivers the results you want.

BEST PRACTICES FOR NEEDS ASSESSMENT

Needs assessment is a critical step in building your Deal Desk, but it's not always easy. Keep these best practices in mind as you go through the process:

1. Involve the right stakeholders: Needs assessment shouldn't be a solo effort. Involve key stakeholders from across the organization, including sales, legal, finance, and operations. This will ensure that you get a diverse range of perspectives and insights and do not miss any of your team's frustrations.

2. Use data to drive decisions: Don't rely on anecdotes or gut feelings alone. Use data and metrics to support your needs assessment and prioritize your requirements. Look at things like deal cycle times, win rates, and average deal sizes to identify areas for improvement.

3. Be realistic about your resources: As you define your goals and requirements, be realistic about the resources you have available to build and maintain your Deal Desk. This includes budget, headcount, and technology. Don't bite off more than you can chew—focus on the most critical needs first and build from there.

4. Communicate and align: Needs assessment is just the beginning of your Deal Desk journey. As you move forward, make sure to communicate your needs and requirements clearly to all stakeholders and ensure

that everyone is aligned with your goals. This will help ensure a smooth and successful implementation.

It is important to remember that you can adapt to change and continuously improve. This principle is crucial in the dynamic world of startups and fast-growing businesses. Your initial needs assessment is not set in stone; it's a living document that should evolve with your organization. As your business grows, market conditions shift, or new technologies emerge, be prepared to revisit and refine your needs assessment.

Implement a regular review process, perhaps quarterly or bi-annually, to reassess your Deal Desk needs. This ongoing evaluation allows you to:

a) Adjust priorities based on changing business goals

b) Incorporate feedback from your team as they use the Deal Desk

c) Identify new areas for improvement or optimization

d) Adapt to new market trends or competitive pressures

e) Leverage emerging technologies that could enhance your Deal Desk operations

Remember, the most successful Deal Desks embrace a culture of continuous improvement. By staying flexible and open to change, you ensure your Deal Desk remains a dynamic, value-driving asset for your organization rather than a static process that quickly becomes outdated.

Illustrative Example: How Acme Corporation Used Needs Assessment to Build a Winning Deal Desk

Let's look at how one company used needs assessment to build a Deal Desk that transformed their business.

Acme Corporation was struggling with a deal management process that was manual, inconsistent, and prone to errors. Deals were taking too long to close, pricing was all over the map, and there was little visibility into the pipeline. The sales team was frustrated, and customers were starting to take their business elsewhere.

Acme knew they needed to make a change, so they embarked on a needs assessment to identify barriers in their processes and define their requirements for a new Deal Desk. Here's how they did it:

Step 1—Map the Current Process

Acme started by mapping out its current deal management process from start to finish. They documented every step, including who was involved, what tools and systems they used, and how long each step typically took.

What they discovered was alarming but not surprising. Their deal process had evolved organically over years of business growth, with new steps added as needs arose but without any holistic redesign. The result was a convoluted web of activities that frustrated everyone involved.

To visualize this complex situation, Acme created a process map that resembled the chaotic collaboration boards many teams use for brainstorming—a fitting representation of their disorganized approach to deal management. This visual mapping exercise was crucial as it transformed vague frustrations into concrete issues that could be addressed systematically.

Figure 1. Inefficient Deal Flow Approval Process (Miro Style)

This diagram visualizes the dysfunctional journey of deals without a Deal Desk, presented as a chaotic Miro board

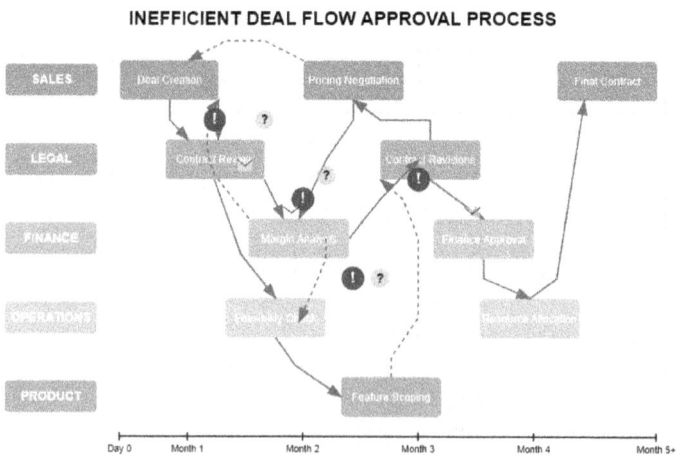

INEFFICIENT DEAL FLOW APPROVAL PROCESS

What the Diagram Shows: The figure presents a collaborative workspace where the deal process has descended into disorder.

Like a Miro board where team members have added elements without coordination, the diagram reveals a tangled web of connections between color-coded department activities, with no central organization or logical progression.

Key Problems Visualized: The mapping exercise revealed several critical issues plaguing Acme's deal process:

Departmental Silos - Teams operated in isolation with their own processes and priorities, creating disconnects during handoffs.

Maze-like Pathways - Deals followed unpredictable routes, often getting trapped in circular patterns of revision and re-approval.

Ownership Confusion - At multiple points, no one clearly owned responsibility for moving deals forward.

Unpredictable Timelines - What should have been a 1-2 month process routinely stretched to 5+ months, with deals spending most of their time waiting rather than being actively worked.

Process Fragmentation - Related activities were scattered throughout the workflow rather than grouped logically, creating inefficiency and confusion.

This visual perfectly captures the reality many organizations face: a deal approval process that evolved without intentional design, resulting in a system that frustrates employees, tests customer patience, and ultimately costs the company revenue through delays, lost deals, and suboptimal terms.

The mapping exercise was eye-opening for Acme's leadership team. It helped them understand why deals were taking so long to close and why sales reps and customers were so frustrated. More importantly, it gave them a baseline against which they could design a better process.

The Deal Desk Solution

After thoroughly analyzing its current state, Acme realized it needed to completely reimagine its deal process. The chaos visualized in Figure 1 couldn't be fixed with minor tweaks— it required a fundamental restructuring with a central coordinating function.

This realization led Acme to design a Deal Desk that would serve as the orchestrator of its entire deal process. Rather than allowing deals to meander through disconnected departments, they created a streamlined workflow with clear phases, decision points, and accountability mechanisms.

Figure 2. Optimized Deal Flow Process

This diagram illustrates a streamlined, transparent deal flow with the Deal Desk as the central orchestrator

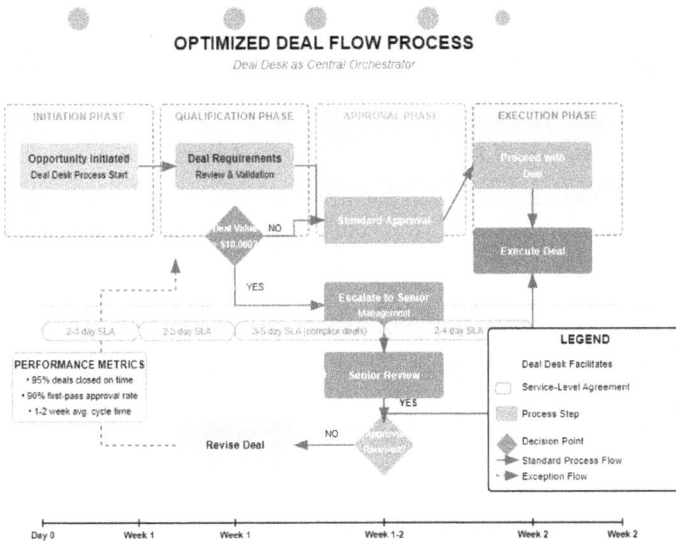

OPTIMIZED DEAL FLOW PROCESS
Deal Desk as Central Orchestrator

What the Diagram Shows: This figure presents a methodical, efficient workflow that transforms the deal process from a source of frustration into a strategic advantage. The Deal Desk serves as the central coordinator, ensuring smooth transitions between clearly defined phases while maintaining consistent communication across all stakeholders.

Key Strengths Visualized:

Phase-Based Organization - The process is divided into four distinct phases (Initiation, Qualification, Approval, and

Execution), each with clear responsibilities and outcomes. This creates natural checkpoints and prevents deals from getting lost between departments.

Value-Based Routing - A clear decision diamond routes deals based on value thresholds ($10,000), ensuring appropriate levels of scrutiny while preventing unnecessary bureaucracy for smaller transactions.

Dedicated Deal Desk Facilitation - Green "DD" markers throughout the process indicate where the Deal Desk actively facilitates transitions, ensuring no deal falls through the cracks even during handoffs between departments.

Clear Service Level Agreements - Blue SLA indicators establish precise timeframes for each phase (2-5 days depending on complexity), creating accountability and allowing for accurate forecasting of deal completion dates.

Transparent Performance Metrics - A metrics panel displays key performance indicators (95% on-time closure, 90% first-pass approval rate, 1-2 week average cycle time), promoting accountability and continuous improvement.

This visual demonstrates how a well-designed Deal Desk transforms chaotic deal management into a strategic advantage. By bringing structure, accountability, and transparency to the process, the organization gains the ability to close deals faster, with greater consistency and improved terms.

The transformation from Figure 1 to Figure 2 wasn't merely cosmetic—it represented a fundamental shift in how Acme approached deal management. The new process eliminated the confusion, delays, and frustration that had previously characterized their deals. More importantly, it created a predictable, efficient system that both internal teams and customers could trust.

In my consulting work, I've seen this transformation repeated across dozens of organizations. While the specific design may vary based on business needs, the core principles remain consistent: centralized coordination, clear ownership, defined service levels, and transparent metrics. When these elements come together in a well-designed Deal Desk, the impact on business performance is both immediate and lasting.

Step 2—Identify Pain Points and Opportunities

Based on their process map, they identified several key constraints, including:

- A manual and time-consuming pricing and quoting process

- Lack of standardization and consistency in contracts and terms

- Poor communication and collaboration between their sales, legal, and finance teams

- Limited visibility into the pipeline and deal status

Acme then dug deeper into their holdups to identify the root causes and potential opportunities for improvement.

For example, they realized that their manual pricing and quoting process was causing delays and errors because sales reps had to enter data manually into multiple systems and wait for approvals from finance. They saw an opportunity to automate this process with a centralized pricing and quoting tool that could integrate with their CRM and ERP systems.

Similarly, they identified an opportunity to standardize their contracts and terms by creating a library of pre-approved clauses and templates that could be easily customized for each deal. This would not only save time but also ensure consistency and reduce legal risk.

Step 3—Define Goals and Requirements

Finally, Acme translated their obstacles and opportunities into clear goals and requirements for their new Deal Desk. Their goals included:

- Reducing average deal cycle time by 30 percent within the next year

- Improving price consistency and accuracy by 95 percent

- Increasing pipeline visibility and deal forecast accuracy to within 5 percent

Their requirements included:

- Automated pricing and quoting tool with CRM and ERP integration

- Centralized contract management system with pre-approved clause library

- Real-time pipeline dashboard with drill-down capabilities

- Cross-functional deal team collaboration tools

With these goals and requirements in hand, Acme could build a Deal Desk that was tailored to their specific needs and designed to deliver actual results. Within the first year of implementation, they had already seen significant improvements in deal cycle times, pricing accuracy, and pipeline visibility. They laid the foundation for a more collaborative, efficient, and customer-centric deal management process for the future.

CONCLUSION

Needs assessment may not be the most glamorous part of building a Deal Desk, but it is arguably the most important. By taking the time to map your current processes, identify your obstacles and opportunities, and define your goals and requirements, you set yourself up for success and ensure that your Deal Desk delivers the results you need.

After thoroughly assessing your Deal Desk needs, it's time to translate those insights into actionable plans. Before we dive into hiring and building your team in the next chapter, let's take a crucial intermediate step: defining your ideal Deal Desk structure and the key roles within it. If you find the assessment process challenging or want an objective, expert perspective, consider leveraging external expertise.

And speaking of Deal Desk excellence (smooth transition, right?), Deal Solutions (dealsolutions. net)—which I may or may not be affiliated with—specializes in helping businesses figure out exactly what they need in this space.

—Deal Solutions Consulting

CHAPTER 5

FROM STRATEGY TO TEAM: BUILDING YOUR DEAL DESK DREAM TEAM

Congratulations! You've completed your thorough needs assessment and have a crystal-clear picture of what you want your Deal Desk to achieve. You're armed with detailed process maps, a list of problems to solve, and a set of SMART goals to guide your path.

With a clear understanding of your needs, the next step is architecting your ideal team structure. This involves defining key roles, outlining responsibilities, and creating job descriptions aligning with your requirements.

1. **Defining Your Deal Desk Structure**

   Based on your needs assessment, determine the optimal structure for your Deal Desk. This could range from a small, agile team for startups to a more complex, multi-tiered structure for larger organizations.

2. **Outlining Key Roles and Responsibilities**

   Identify the critical roles needed to fulfill your Deal Desk functions. Depending on your needs and budget, this might include positions like Director, Manager, or Analyst. For each role, clearly define the primary responsibilities, required skills, and how they contribute to your overall Deal Desk strategy.

3. **Creating Comprehensive Job Descriptions**

   Create detailed job descriptions for each role, ensuring they reflect the technical and soft skills required for success in your unique Deal Desk environment.

4. **Aligning Roles with Your Growth Strategy**

   Ensure that your planned team structure can scale with your organization's growth. Consider how roles might evolve over time and what additional positions you might need in the future.

With this strategic groundwork laid, you're now ready to begin the exciting process of bringing your Deal Desk dream team to life. Let's dive into the art and science of recruiting, hiring, and onboarding the right talent to drive your Deal Desk success.

Now, it's time to build the team that will make your Deal Desk dreams a reality.

Assembling your Deal Desk team is like casting the characters for a blockbuster movie. Each role is critical, and the chemistry between team members can make or break the production. You need a mix of superstars and supporting actors, each bringing their unique talents and expertise. Just like in Hollywood, finding the right fit takes time, effort, and a bit of luck.

Get busy living, or get busy dying.

—*The Shawshank Redemption*

But fear not, aspiring Deal Desk director. I'll show you how to build your elite Deal Desk team—covering essential roles, critical skills, and proven hiring strategies. You'll learn exactly what it takes to assemble a team that elevates your entire deal management process.

You're the director of a high-stakes blockbuster, and your film's success hinges on assembling the perfect cast. But this isn't just any Hollywood production—it's your Deal Desk, and the stars you choose will make or break your business's ability to close deals and drive revenue.

Just like the movies, building a high-performing Deal Desk team is both an art and a science. It requires a keen eye for talent, a deep understanding of the skills and qualities needed for each role, and a commitment to nurturing and developing your cast. And just like in Hollywood, you need to look beyond the glitz and glamour to find the true superstars—the transformational leaders with high emotional intelligence who can elevate your Deal Desk from a box office flop to a critical and commercial success.

Let's take a look behind the scenes of the Deal Desk casting process and explore the key roles and responsibilities of your dream team, the skills and qualities to look for in your leads, and the best practices for auditioning, onboarding, and developing your cast. We'll also delve into the importance of transformational leadership and emotional intelligence in driving Deal Desk success and show you how to spot the Oscar-worthy performers who can take your team to new levels of success.

So, grab your director's chair and get ready to shout "Action!"— it's time to assemble the cast of your Deal Desk dreams.

THE LEADING ROLES: KEY PLAYERS IN YOUR DEAL DESK CAST

Before you hold auditions, it's important to understand the key roles and responsibilities of your Deal Desk cast. While every production is different, a few leading roles are essential to any Deal Desk blockbuster:

1. The Director: Deal Desk Manager

    ⁄ Responsibilities:

    ◆ Lead the overall Deal Desk strategy and operations

    ◆ Manage the cast and ensure alignment with broader business goals

- ◆ Continuously optimize the Deal Desk process and technology

⟋ Skills and Qualities:

- ◆ Strong leadership and communication skills

- ◆ Deep understanding of the sales process and deal management best practices

- ◆ Ability to think strategically and make data-driven decisions

2. The Lead Actor: Pricing and Deal Strategist

⟋ Responsibilities:

- ◆ Develop and maintain pricing models and strategies

- ◆ Analyze deal profitability and make recommendations for optimization

- ◆ Collaborate with sales to structure complex deals and negotiate terms

⟋ Skills and Qualities:

- ◆ Analytical and data-savvy

- ◆ Strong business acumen and understanding of market dynamics

- ◆ Excellent communication and collaboration skills

3. The Supporting Actor: Contract and Legal Specialist

, Responsibilities:

◆ Review and approve contracts and legal documents

◆ Ensure compliance with legal and regulatory requirements

◆ Manage contract lifecycle and track key milestones and obligations

, Skills and Qualities:

◆ Deep knowledge of contract law and regulatory landscape

◆ Detail-oriented and process-driven

◆ Ability to balance risk management with business needs

4. The Stunt Coordinator: Order Processing and Fulfillment Coordinator

, Responsibilities:

◆ Manage order processing and fulfillment workflows

◆ Coordinate with internal teams and external partners to ensure timely delivery

◆ Track and report on key fulfillment metrics and service level agreements (SLAs)

, Skills and Qualities:

- ◆ Strong project management and coordination skills

- ◆ Attention to detail and ability to manage multiple priorities

- ◆ Customer-centric mindset and commitment to excellence

5. The Script Supervisor: Deal Desk Analyst

 ⁄ Responsibilities:

- ◆ Analyze deal data and generate insights and reports

- ◆ Monitor key Deal Desk metrics and identify areas for improvement

- ◆ Supports data-driven decision-making across the cast

⁄ Skills and Qualities:

- ◆ Strong analytical and problem-solving skills

- ◆ Proficiency with data analysis tools and techniques

- ◆ Ability to communicate complex data in clear and actionable ways

In an ideal scenario, a specialist would fill each of these roles. However, the reality for many startups and growing businesses is that your Deal Desk might start with just one or two key players. In fact, your first hire might need to be a

Jack-of-all-trades (or, as I like to say, a Jill-of-all-trades), capable of wearing multiple hats and juggling diverse responsibilities.

When you're working with a limited headcount, it's crucial to find individuals who possess a broad skill set and can adapt to various aspects of the Deal Desk's function and needs. This versatile professional should have a working knowledge of pricing strategies, legal considerations, financial analysis, and operational processes. They should be comfortable interfacing with sales teams while also managing the nitty-gritty of deal structures.

Keep in mind that some functions, such as orders and bookings, might be handled by separate departments depending on your organizational structure. The key is to ensure your Deal Desk, whether it's a team of one or many, has the right blend of skills and expertise to drive deal success.

As your business grows and deal complexity increases, you can gradually expand your team, bringing in specialists for each core function. But in the early stages, prioritize finding adaptable, multi-skilled professionals who can lay a sound foundation for your Deal Desk operations. Remember, in the world of startups and high-growth companies, versatility can be just as valuable as specialization.

THE IMPORTANCE OF TRANSFORMATIONAL LEADERSHIP AND EMOTIONAL INTELLIGENCE (EQ)

(More details on EQ in Part 5: After Credits—The Human Element: Building a World-Class Deal Desk Culture)

In the world of Hollywood, there are actors who can deliver a line, and then there are actors who can bring a character to life. The difference often lies in their ability to connect with the audience on an emotional level, to inspire and move them in ways that transcend the script.

The same is true in the world of Deal Desks. While technical skills and expertise are essential, true superstars are transformational leaders with high emotional intelligence—the ones who can inspire and motivate their teams to achieve greatness, even in the face of complex challenges and high-pressure situations.

Transformational leaders are the visionaries of the Deal Desk world. They have a clear sense of purpose and direction and can articulate that vision in a way that inspires and motivates others. They're also willing to challenge the status quo and take risks in pursuit of innovation and growth.

Transformational leadership is about combining big-picture thinking with emotional intelligence. Emotionally intelligent leaders have a deep understanding of their own emotions and the emotions of others, and they use that understanding to build trust, foster collaboration, and navigate complex social dynamics.

Emotional intelligence is critical for success in a Deal Desk context. Deals can be high-stakes and highly emotional, with multiple stakeholders and competing priorities. A leader with high emotional intelligence can read the room, anticipate potential conflicts, and adjust their approach accordingly.

They can also create a culture of psychological safety, where team members feel comfortable taking risks, admitting mistakes, and challenging assumptions.

So, as you cast your Deal Desk blockbuster, don't just look for technical skills and expertise. Look for transformational leaders with high emotional intelligence—the ones who can take your team to the next level and create a Deal Desk that's truly worthy of the red-carpet treatment.

THE AUDITION PROCESS: FINDING YOUR DEAL DESK SUPERSTARS

Now that you know what kind of cast you're looking for, let the auditions begin. Let's find your Deal Desk superstars! But just like in Hollywood, finding the right talent takes more than just posting a casting call and hoping for the best. Use these tips and best practices for auditioning and selecting your dream team:

1. Look for range and versatility

    In Hollywood, the best actors are the ones who can play a wide range of roles and adapt to different genres and styles. The same is true for your Deal Desk cast. Look for candidates who have experience across multiple functions and industries and can adapt to new challenges and opportunities as they arise.

    Pay particular attention to candidates who have successfully navigated complex deals or high-pressure situations in the past. These are the actors who can improvise and think on their feet when the script goes off the rails. Include interview questions designed to identify candidates who have these skills.

2. Conduct a case study activity for the final candidate(s)

   You can assess how well candidates communicate, problem-solve, and present their ideas during the interview process.

   If you are hiring more than one person, consider conducting group interviews or case studies that require candidates to work together to solve a problem or develop a strategy. Pay attention to how they interact, share ideas, and resolve conflicts—these are all key indicators of their ability to work effectively as part of a high-performing cast.

3. Look for emotional intelligence and transformational leadership potential

   As discussed, transformational leadership and emotional intelligence are critical qualities for Deal Desk success. Look for candidates who show these qualities in their past experiences and their interactions with you and other cast members.

   Ask behavioral questions that probe for examples of how candidates have inspired and motivated teams, navigated complex social dynamics, and created a culture of trust and collaboration. The best actors are the ones who can bring out the best in their co-stars and create a whole that is greater than the sum of its parts.

4. Build a dynamic team (See Part 5 for more detailed information)

    Creating a high-performing Deal Desk team requires bringing together professionals with varied perspectives, skill sets, and experiences. Look for candidates who can contribute unique insights and approaches while fostering a collaborative, welcoming environment where all team members can thrive.

    Consider implementing objective hiring practices and partnering with professional organizations to expand your talent pool and reach qualified candidates from all backgrounds. A team that brings together different viewpoints and experiences will be better equipped to tackle complex deal management challenges and drive organizational success.

5. Trust your instincts

    At the end of the day, casting is as much an art as a science. Just like a great director, you need to trust your instincts and go with your gut when selecting your Deal Desk cast.

    Look for candidates who have that "it" factor—the ones who light up the room and make you feel excited about the possibilities of what your team can achieve together. These are the superstars who will help you create a Deal Desk blockbuster that will be the talk of the industry.

ROLLING OUT THE RED CARPET: EMPOWER YOUR NEW HIRE TO SHAPE THE DEAL DESK

Congratulations, director—you've assembled an A-list cast ready to take your deal operations to the next level! But your work is just beginning. Now it's time to roll out the red carpet and give your new hire(s) the star treatment they deserve.

When bringing on your first Deal Desk hire, it's crucial to understand that this individual will play a pivotal role in shaping and developing your Deal Desk function. Unlike established departments, a new Deal Desk often requires a pioneering spirit and the ability to build processes from the ground up.

1. Share Existing Knowledge and Documentation

    Provide your new hire with any current processes, documentation, and insights about your sales organization. This gives them a starting point and context for understanding your business.

2. Set Clear Expectations for Process Development

    Communicate that a crucial part of their role will be to assess, develop, and implement Deal Desk processes. They should expect to create a comprehensive plan for building out the Deal Desk function.

3. Encourage Collaboration with Sales and Other Departments

   The new hire should work closely with your sales team and other relevant departments to understand pain points, inefficiencies, and opportunities for improvement in the current deal process.

4. Support Iterative Process Creation

   Understand that creating effective Deal Desk processes is often an iterative process. Encourage your new hire to start with basic frameworks and refine them based on real-world application and feedback.

5. Facilitate On-the-Job Learning

   While formal training may be limited initially, you can facilitate hands-on learning opportunities. This could involve shadowing sales calls, participating in deal negotiations, or analyzing past deals.

6. Invest in Relevant Tools and Resources

   Work with your new hire or hires to identify and invest in the tools and resources they'll need to build an effective Deal Desk. This might include CRM systems, contract management software, or analytics platforms.

7. Foster a Culture of Continuous Improvement

Encourage your new hire to evaluate and improve Deal Desk processes continuously. This might involve regular check-ins, performance metrics, and a willingness to adapt based on results.

Remember, building a Deal Desk from scratch is a significant undertaking. Your new hire will be instrumental in laying the foundation, creating processes, and supporting your sales organization. Provide them with the support, resources, and autonomy they need to succeed in this crucial role. As the Deal Desk evolves, they'll be able to develop more structured training and onboarding processes for future team members.

A virtual Deal Desk can be an excellent solution for businesses not ready to commit to full-time hires or for those seeking flexibility. Deal Solutions provides virtual Deal Desk services, allowing you to access expert deal management support without the overhead of an in-house team.

FROM PILOT TO BLOCKBUSTER: EVOLVING YOUR DEAL DESK FOR LONG-TERM SUCCESS

You've brought on your Deal Desk pioneer, laid the groundwork, and gotten your Deal Desk off to a promising start. But just like in the world of startups, the true test of your success will be how well your Deal Desk evolves and scales over time. Will it remain a solo performance, or will it grow into an ensemble cast delivering consistent value year after year?

The key to long-term Deal Desk success is fostering a culture of continuous improvement and adaptation. Consider these strategies for developing your Deal Desk:

1. Foster a Learning Organization

    ⁞ Encourage your Deal Desk team to stay ahead of the curve by continuously learning about new technologies, best practices, and industry trends.

    ⁞ As the team grows, consider developing an internal 'Deal Desk Academy' where team members can share knowledge, discuss challenges, and collaboratively solve problems.

    ⁞ Encourage team members to attend relevant conferences and webinars or pursue certifications that enhance their skills and bring new insights to the team.

2. Encourage Cross-Functional Collaboration

    ⁞ As your Deal Desk evolves, it's crucial to maintain strong relationships with other departments. Encourage your team to regularly collaborate with sales, legal, finance, and other key stakeholders.

    ⁞ Consider implementing a 'rotation program' where Deal Desk team members can spend time in other departments to gain a more holistic understanding of the business.

    ⁞ Host regular cross-functional meetings or workshops to ensure alignment and share best practices across the organization.

3. Implement a Mentorship Program

   › As your team grows, establish a mentorship program where more experienced team members can guide and support newer additions.

   › This not only helps in knowledge transfer but also maintains the pioneering spirit and problem-solving attitude that was crucial in the early days of your Deal Desk.

4. Cultivate Innovation and Experimentation

   › Encourage your team to question and improve existing processes continuously. What worked in the early days may need refinement as the business scales.

   › Set aside time for 'innovation sprints' where team members can propose and test new ideas for improving Deal Desk operations.

   › Celebrate both successes and 'productive failures'—learning from what doesn't work is just as important as replicating what does.

5. Develop a Robust Feedback Loop

   › Implement regular check-ins with the sales team and other stakeholders to ensure the Deal Desk is continually meeting the evolving needs of the business.

   › Use data and analytics to track the impact of the Deal Desk on key metrics like deal velocity, win rates, and revenue. Use these insights to guide future improvements.

6. Recognize and Reward Growth

⟩ Celebrate team members who drive significant improvements, take on new challenges, or achieve important milestones.

⟩ Consider creating a 'Deal Desk Innovator of the Year' award or similar recognition program to highlight exceptional contributions.

Remember, building a successful Deal Desk is a journey, not a destination. By fostering a culture of continuous learning, collaboration, and innovation, you'll ensure that your Deal Desk doesn't just survive but thrives, delivering increasing value to your organization as it grows and evolves.

FROM BLOCKBUSTER TO BOX OFFICE SMASH: YOUR DEAL DESK JOURNEY BEGINS

Congratulations, visionary founder! You've taken the crucial first step by bringing on your Deal Desk pioneer, laying the groundwork for what promises to be a game-changing addition to your startup. You've set the stage for success but remember—this is just the pilot episode of what could be an award-winning series.

As you move forward, keep in mind that your Deal Desk isn't a static entity but a dynamic force that will grow and evolve with your business. Stay agile, remain open to pivoting, and always be ready to iterate on your processes. The most successful startups are those that adapt quickly to changing market conditions and internal needs.

Your initial Deal Desk hire is not just an employee but a co-creator of this critical function within your organization. Empower them with the resources they need, but also give them the autonomy to shape the role and its impact on your business. Trust in their expertise, but don't be afraid to challenge assumptions and push for innovation.

As your Deal Desk grows from a one-person show into an ensemble cast, remember that each new addition brings fresh perspectives and potential for growth. Encourage your team to stay curious, question the status quo, and always seek ways to drive more value for your organization.

The startup world moves fast, and your Deal Desk needs to move even faster. Keep your finger on the pulse of industry trends, emerging technologies, and evolving best practices. Be ready to pivot your strategies as needed, and don't be afraid to take calculated risks in pursuit of breakthrough improvements.

So, are you ready to take your startup to the next level? Your Deal Desk journey is just beginning, and the potential is limitless. It's time to show the world how a well-crafted Deal Desk can be the secret weapon that propels a startup from scrappy underdog to industry leader.

Lights, camera, action! Let's make your Deal Desk the star of your startup's success story!

CHAPTER 6

EQUIPPING YOUR DEAL DESK FOR BOX OFFICE SUCCESS WITH TECH AND TOOLS OF THE TRADE

You've assembled your dream cast, and they're ready to take the Deal Desk world by storm. But just like in Hollywood, even the most talented actors need the right tools and technology to bring their performances to life on the big screen.

In the world of Deal Desks, technology is the secret weapon that can transform your team from a scrappy indie production into a box office sensation. The modern Deal Desk leverages a powerful combination of traditional software and cutting-edge artificial intelligence (AI) tools to streamline operations and drive unprecedented efficiency.

From robust CRM systems and contract management software to advanced data analytics and project management platforms, the foundation of your tech stack remains crucial. However, the game-changer in today's landscape is the integration of AI-powered tools. These innovative solutions can automate complex processes, offer predictive insights, and supercharge your team's capabilities.

Imagine AI algorithms that can predict deal outcomes with uncanny accuracy and models that optimize pricing strategies in real time. Visualize AI tools that can review and flag potential issues in contracts within seconds or AI-powered chatbots that can handle routine deal inquiries, freeing up your team for more strategic work.

Imagine you're using outdated software, and it feels like trying to run a marathon in flip-flops. Now, imagine switching to a tool that's built for speed and efficiency. That's the power of using the right technology for the right purpose.

Sometimes you gotta run before you can walk.

—*Iron Man*

While Tony was talking about testing his Iron Man suit, this principle has proven true in my own life—particularly during a defining moment in my diving career that taught me valuable lessons about taking calculated risks and adapting under pressure.

Picture this: I was a sophomore at Michigan State University, and I got an unexpected offer to perform in professional diving shows on an International High Diving Team at a water park in France. The catch? I hadn't been on a diving board in months. After not making the MSU team in my second year (our Olympic diver rightfully commanded the coach's attention), my diving muscles had grown rusty. But sometimes, the best opportunities come when you're least "ready" for them.

When I arrived in France, I faced a challenge that would make most divers balk: a pool that seemed more suited for a backyard in Michigan than professional diving shows. At just three meters deep—far shallower than regulation diving pools—our team was expected to perform from heights of three, ten, fifteen, and even twenty-five meters. To put this in perspective, imagine trying to land a plane on a runway half its usual length. That's essentially what we were doing but with our bodies as the aircraft and the shallow pool as our abbreviated landing strip. The margin for error was microscopic, and the consequences of a miscalculation were serious. This wasn't just about performing; it was about adapting our techniques for safety while delivering an exceptional show. See photos below:

Figure 1. Idea of the size of the pool. Three-meter boards and ten-meter platforms are showing with people on them. The fifteen-meter platform is visible. The twenty-five-meter platform is out of frame.

Figure 2. I am the female over the bottom right gentleman.

Figure 3: I am the only female on the left on the three-meter board. This photo shows where we all dive into the pool simultaneously.

The conventional wisdom would have been to start small, gradually working our way up to the higher platforms. But we didn't have that luxury. The shows were starting, and the audience didn't care about our practice time—they wanted a spectacle. I had to trust my fundamentals, adapt quickly, and quite literally dive in.

This experience taught me three crucial lessons that I've carried into the world of Deal Desks:

1. Trust Your Foundation

   Just as my years of diving training gave me the fundamental skills to adapt to that shallow pool, your business experience provides the foundation for implementing a Deal Desk. You don't need to have every process perfected before you start.

2. Adapt to Constraints

   That three-meter-deep pool forced us to be precise in our movements and adjust our entries to immediately flip or scoop (depending on headfirst or feetfirst landing, respectively) underwater to avoid hitting the bottom. Similarly, your Deal Desk might need to work within tight time, resources, or personnel constraints. The key is not to wait for perfect conditions but to adapt and excel within your limitations.

3. Calculate Your Risks

   While diving into a shallow pool from 25 meters might sound reckless, it was actually a carefully calculated risk. We knew our capabilities and adjusted our techniques accordingly. Your Deal Desk implementation might seem daunting, but with proper preparation and awareness of your capabilities, you can take bold steps safely.

Those two summers in France taught me that sometimes you must take the plunge before feeling completely ready. In the world of Deal Desks, waiting for perfect conditions or complete preparation can mean missing crucial opportunities for growth. Just as I had to trust my training and adapt to challenging conditions in that French water park, you'll need to trust your business acumen and adapt your Deal Desk to your unique circumstances.

Remember: The goal isn't to be perfect from day one—it's to start strong and keep improving. Just like a diver adjusting their entry angle for a shallow pool, you'll fine-tune your Deal Desk processes as you go. The key is to begin with confidence, knowing that your business fundamentals will help you navigate the challenges ahead.

In diving, we had to master both technique and technology— from understanding water dynamics to using video analysis to improve our form. Similarly, your Deal Desk success depends on blending fundamental business practices with modern tools. With the right combination of traditional software and AI tools, your Deal Desk can automate manual processes, gain real-time insights, and empower your team to work more efficiently and effectively than ever before. This technological edge doesn't just level the playing field—it propels your Deal

Desk into a league of its own, ready to tackle the most complex deals with the finesse of a seasoned Hollywood producer.

But with so many options out there, how do you choose the right tools for your Deal Desk? And once you have them, how do you ensure your team is using them to their full potential? Let's explore the tech and tools of the Deal Desk trade and discover how to equip your team for blockbuster success.

THE ESSENTIAL TOOLS OF THE TRADE: BLENDING TRADITIONAL SOFTWARE WITH THE INNOVATION OF AI

Just as a modern filmmaker needs both classic equipment and cutting-edge technology, your Deal Desk requires a mix of traditional software and AI-powered tools to operate at peak efficiency. Here's an updated toolkit for the AI-enhanced Deal Desk:

1. AI-Integrated Customer Relationship Management (CRM) System

   - A CRM system remains the foundation of any high-performing Deal Desk, but now with AI capabilities.

   - Look for CRMs with AI features like predictive lead scoring, automated data entry, and intelligent forecasting. Options include DealHub, Salesforce Einstein, or HubSpot's AI tools.

   - Ultimately, you want a flexible CRM that can adapt to changes swiftly.

2. AI-Powered Configure, Price, Quote (CPQ) Software

   , Modern CPQ software leverages AI to revolutionize complex pricing and quoting scenarios.

   , Seek CPQ solutions with AI-driven pricing optimization, product recommendations, and approval automation. Consider DealHub or Salesforce CPQ with Einstein.

3. AI-Enhanced Contract Lifecycle Management (CLM) System

   , AI is transforming CLM systems, making contract management faster and more accurate.

   , Look for CLMs with AI capabilities like automatic contract analysis, risk identification, and clause recommendation. Options include DealHub, Ironclad, Icertis, Evasort, or Ariba.

4. AI-Driven Business Intelligence and Analytics Platform

   , AI takes business intelligence to new heights, offering predictive analytics and automated insights.

   , Explore platforms with AI features such as anomaly detection, natural language querying, and automated data preparation. Consider Tableau with Einstein Analytics, Microsoft Power BI with AI capabilities, or ThoughtSpot.

5. AI Chatbots and Virtual Assistants

  , A recent addition to the Deal Desk toolkit, AI
    chatbots can handle routine customer inquiries
    and tasks.

  , Look for solutions that can integrate with your
    CRM and other systems to provide real-time deal
    information and basic support. Options include
    Intercom, Drift, or custom solutions built on
    platforms like IBM Watson or Google Cloud AI.

6. AI-Powered Deal Analytics and Forecasting Tools

  , These specialized tools use AI to provide deep
    insights into deal health and likely outcomes.

  , Consider solutions that offer deal risk assessment,
    win probability forecasting, and next-best-action
    recommendations. Examples include Clari,
    InsightSquared, or Aviso.

DATA INTEGRATION AND CENTRALIZATION: THE KEY TO HOLISTIC DEAL INSIGHTS

While each of these tools serves a crucial function, their
true power is unlocked when they work in concert. To
get a complete and accurate picture of your Deal Desk's
performance, you need to centralize and integrate data from
all these sources into a single source of truth.

This integration is critical because it:

1. Eliminates data silos: When information is scattered across different systems, it's difficult to get a holistic view of your deal processes and outcomes.

2. Ensures data consistency: When all teams work from the same integrated dataset, you reduce the risk of discrepancies and miscommunications.

3. Enables more sophisticated analytics: By bringing all your data together, you can perform cross-functional analyses that reveal deeper insights about your deal processes and outcomes.

4. Supports real-time decision-making: With a centralized, integrated data source, you can create dashboards and reports that give stakeholders up-to-the-minute insights on deal progress and performance.

5. Facilitates automation: Integrated systems can more easily share data and trigger automated workflows, further streamlining your deal processes.

When selecting these tools, prioritize solutions that offer robust integration capabilities and align with your specific Deal Desk needs. Look for pre-built connectors between your chosen platforms, or ensure that they have well-documented application programming interfaces (APIs) that will allow for custom integrations. The goal is to create a cohesive ecosystem where AI enhances every aspect of your deal management process, from initial customer contact to final contract signature.

Remember, the goal is to create a seamless flow of information across your entire deal lifecycle. This not only makes your Deal Desk more efficient, but also positions it as a strategic asset that can provide valuable insights to the entire organization. While AI tools can dramatically improve efficiency and provide valuable insights, they're most effective when combined with human expertise. Your team's experience and judgment remain crucial in interpreting AI-generated insights and making strategic decisions.

CHOOSING THE RIGHT TOOLS FOR YOUR DEAL DESK

Navigating the vast landscape of available technologies for your Deal Desk can be as complex as designing a groundbreaking product. The choices you make will significantly impact your team's efficiency and effectiveness. To ensure you select the optimal tools for your specific needs, consider these key factors:

1. Alignment with your needs and goals

     Before evaluating, clearly define your Deal Desk's unique requirements and strategic objectives. Use these as your guiding stars throughout the selection process.

2. Ease of use and adoption

> Even the most powerful tool is ineffective if your team won't use it. Prioritize intuitive interfaces and user-friendly designs that will encourage widespread adoption.

3. Integration and compatibility

> Your Deal Desk tools should work seamlessly together, creating a cohesive ecosystem rather than a patchwork of isolated solutions. Look for robust integration capabilities with your existing systems. If your team needs to enter information manually from one system into another for your Deal Desk to function, it's a recipe for delays and disasters.

4. Scalability and flexibility

> As your Deal Desk evolves, your tools should grow with you. Opt for solutions that can adapt to changing needs and handle increasing complexity over time.

5. AI and automation capabilities

> In today's tech-driven landscape, AI-powered features can provide a significant competitive edge. Consider how each tool leverages AI to automate tasks, provide insights, and enhance decision-making.

By carefully weighing these factors, you can build a technology stack that not only meets your current needs but also positions your Deal Desk for future success and innovation.

IMPLEMENTING AND ADOPTING YOUR DEAL DESK TOOLS

You've chosen your tools, and you're ready to roll. But just like a new piece of equipment on a film set, your Deal Desk tools won't do you any good if your team doesn't know how to use them effectively. Use these best practices for implementing and adopting your new technologies:

1. Develop a comprehensive implementation plan

    > Before you roll out your new tools, take the time to develop a comprehensive implementation plan that outlines your goals, timeline, and resources. Consider factors like data migration, integration with existing systems, and training and support for your team.

    > Assign clear roles and responsibilities for the implementation process and communicate regularly with your team and stakeholders to keep everyone informed and aligned.

2. Provide training and support

    > Your team won't be able to use your new tools effectively if they don't know how. Provide comprehensive training and support to help your team learn and adopt your new technologies.

⟋ Consider factors like in-person training sessions, online tutorials and documentation, and ongoing support and troubleshooting. The more supported your team feels, the more likely they are to embrace your new tools and use them to their full potential.

3. Encourage user feedback and adoption

⟋ Your team's feedback and adoption are critical to the success of your new tools. Encourage your team to provide feedback on their experience with the new technologies and use that feedback to improve and optimize your processes.

⟋ Consider factors like user surveys, focus groups, and adoption metrics. The more engaged your team is with your new tools, the more value you'll get out of them in the long run.

4. Celebrate successes and milestones

⟋ Implementing new tools and technologies can be a big undertaking, and it's important to celebrate your successes and milestones along the way. Take the time to recognize and reward your team for their hard work and achievements.

⟋ Consider factors like project milestones, user adoption metrics, and overall business impact. The more you celebrate your successes, the more motivated your team will be to keep pushing forward and making the most of your new tools.

ACTION: PUTTING YOUR DEAL DESK TOOLS TO WORK

Congratulations, director—you've equipped your Deal Desk with the tools and technologies they need to take their performance to the next level. But just like a new camera or special effects rig, your tools are only as good as the way you use them. Use these few tips for putting your Deal Desk tools to work and driving blockbuster results:

1. Use your tools to automate and streamline processes

    ⌐ One of the biggest benefits of Deal Desk tools is their ability to automate manual processes and streamline workflows. Look for opportunities to use your tools to eliminate repetitive tasks, reduce errors, and speed up your deal cycles.

    ⌐ Consider factors like automated data entry, approval workflows, and contract generation. The more you can automate, the more time your team will have to focus on higher-value activities like relationship building and strategic planning.

2. Leverage your data for insights and optimization

    ⌐ Your Deal Desk tools are a gold mine of data and insights that can help you optimize your processes and make data-driven decisions. Use your business intelligence and analytics platform to capture, analyze, and visualize your deal data in real-time.

⟋ Consider factors like deal velocity, win rates, pricing trends, and customer segmentation. The more insights you can glean from your data, the better equipped you'll be to identify areas for improvement and drive better business outcomes.

3. Collaborate and communicate across teams and systems

⟋ Your Deal Desk tools are only as powerful as the way you use them to collaborate and communicate across your organization. Use your tools to break down silos, share information, and work together more effectively.

⟋ Consider factors like shared data and documents, real-time notifications and alerts, and cross-functional workflows. The more you can use your tools to facilitate collaboration and communication, the more aligned and effective your Deal Desk will be.

4. Continuously improve and innovate

⟋ Your Deal Desk tools and processes should never stop evolving and improving. Use your tools to monitor and measure your performance continuously, identify areas for improvement, and test new ideas and approaches.

⟋ Regularly seek user feedback from various groups and share best practices among the stakeholders. The more you can use your tools to drive continuous improvement and innovation, the more competitive and successful your Deal Desk will be in the long run.

THAT'S A WRAP: THE POWER OF THE RIGHT TECH AND TOOLS

And that's a wrap, folks! Just like a diver needs both skill and proper equipment to execute the perfect dive, you've learned about the essential tools of the Deal Desk trade, how to choose the right technologies for your team, and how to implement and adopt them for maximum impact. You've seen how the right tools and technologies can take your Deal Desk from a low-budget indie flick to a big-budget blockbuster, driving automation, insights, collaboration, and continuous improvement.

But remember, director, your tools are only as good as the way you use them. Like that shallow pool in France taught me, it's not about having the perfect conditions—it's about adapting and maximizing what you have. It's up to you to create a culture and environment where you encourage and empower your team to make the most of your technologies and continuously push the boundaries of what's possible. Sometimes you'll need to adjust your approach, just as we adjusted our diving techniques, but with the right tools in place and the right mindset to match, there's no limit to what your Deal Desk can achieve.

So go forth and conquer, director. The Deal Desk world is your oyster, and with the right tech and tools by your side, you're ready to take on whatever challenges come your way.

Just like landing that perfect dive in a challenging pool, it's about having the right equipment, the right mindset, and the confidence to execute. Who knows—maybe one day they'll make a movie about your Deal Desk's rise to fame and fortune. And when they do, you can bet your bottom dollar that technology will play a starring role.

PART 3

OPERATING YOUR DEAL DESK

CHAPTER 7

DEFINING PROCESSES AND WORKFLOWS: CHOREOGRAPHING THE DANCE OF THE DEAL

As a startup leader, you've taken a significant step by recognizing the need for a Deal Desk. You've hired your Deal Desk pioneer or are preparing to do so. Now, it's time to ensure they have the framework to succeed. One of the most critical elements they'll need to develop is a set of clear processes and workflows.

Think of your Deal Desk as a new production your company is launching. Your Deal Desk leader is the director, and each team member they bring on board will be like a performer with a unique role and skill set. The tools and technologies you provide are like the stage and props. However, without a clear and well-defined process for how all these elements come together, even the most talented team with the best tools could result in chaos rather than a smooth, efficient operation.

Your role is to understand the importance of these processes and to support your Deal Desk leader in developing them. Encourage them to design workflows that will allow their team to move in harmony, each person knowing exactly when and how to play their part. This is what will transform your Deal Desk from a concept into a cohesive, high-performing unit capable of handling complex deals with precision.

We will explore the crucial processes and workflows your Deal Desk leader should consider implementing. By understanding these concepts, you'll be better equipped to support their efforts and ensure your Deal Desk performs like a well-orchestrated production, turning potential chaos into a beautiful, efficient operation that drives your business forward.

Remember, while your Deal Desk leader will be the one implementing these processes, your support and understanding of their importance are crucial to the success of this new function in your startup.

The same principle applies to your startup's Deal Desk. No matter how talented your Deal Desk leader is or how cutting-edge the technology you've provided, without clear and well-defined processes and workflows, they'll struggle to achieve the efficiency, consistency, and excellence that defines a high-performing Deal Desk.

As Friedrich Nietzsche wisely said, "He who would learn to fly one day must first learn to stand and walk and run and climb and dance; one cannot fly into flying." At first glance, this might seem to contradict Tony Stark's philosophy that 'sometimes you've got to run before you can walk.' But in the world of Deal Desks, both insights hold true. While there are moments when you need to take bold leaps—like my dive into that shallow French pool—there's also wisdom to building a strong foundation. This quote perfectly encapsulates the methodical journey your Deal Desk will undertake. Your Deal Desk leader can't simply leap into high performance—they need to build a solid foundation of processes and workflows first.

This truth hit home during my transition from Adobe to Forescout Technologies. After years of managing Adobe's Commercial West, Education, and Retail Deal Desk, I thought moving to a cybersecurity company would be straightforward—maybe even easier. After all, I was going from handling hundreds of Adobe products to what I assumed would be a simpler portfolio of cybersecurity solutions. "How hard could it be?" I thought to myself.

That assumption quickly proved naive. While I had mastered the art of software licensing at Adobe, Forescout's business model was a completely different beast. I had to learn the intricacies of hardware sales with and without software, navigate complex licensing models I'd never encountered before, and manage an unexpectedly large array of SKUs that varied by licensing model, partner type, and security modules. Despite my years of Deal Desk expertise, I needed to learn to 'walk' in this new environment before I could 'run.'

Your role as a startup leader is to understand this progression and support your Deal Desk leader through each stage. Just as I had to take time to master new fundamentals at Forescout, encourage your team to develop these foundational elements, even if it means a slightly slower start. In the long run, this methodical approach will enable your Deal Desk to soar, handling complex deals gracefully and driving significant value for your business. Just like mastering a dance routine, building a successful Deal Desk team involves more than just learning the steps. It's about fostering a culture of continuous improvement, encouraging innovation, and instilling a sense of purpose and passion in your team members. This approach not only enhances individual performance but also drives the overall success of the Deal Desk.

It's time to explore the art and science of defining Deal Desk processes and workflows and look at the key elements of effective process design, the best practices for documenting and communicating your processes, and the strategies for continuously improving and optimizing your workflows. With those in place, you'll have a clear roadmap for choreographing the dance of the deal and taking your Deal Desk performance to new heights.

To illustrate the transformative power of well-defined processes and workflows, let's check back in with our friend Olivia from HydroSmarte. Her journey from process chaos to Deal Desk symphony perfectly encapsulates why this step is so crucial.

THE HYDROSMARTE REVOLUTION: OLIVIA'S PROCESS PARADIGM SHIFT

Remember our friend Olivia from HydroSmarte? Well, buckle up because she's back with a vengeance, and she's about to show us how defining the right processes can turn chaos into a symphony of success.

Fast forward: It had been a year since Olivia implemented her Deal Desk, and HydroSmarte had been growing faster than a bamboo shoot in spring. But with growth comes growing pains, and Olivia found herself facing a new challenge: process pandemonium.

One fateful Tuesday, Olivia walked into the office to find her sales team in an uproar. Three different reps had promised three different clients the same "exclusive" pricing on a bulk order of HydroSmarte bottles. The finance team was pulling their hair out over inconsistent discount approvals, and legal was drowning in a sea of non-standard contract terms.

Olivia took a deep breath, channeling her inner Mel Robbins. "Five, four, three, two, one," she counted down silently. Then she sprang into action.

She gathered her team and said, "Folks, it's time for a process makeover. We're going to Marie Kondo our deal workflow!"

Over the next week, Olivia and her team mapped out every step of their deal process, from initial customer contact to final signature. They identified holdups, redundancies, and gaps. To resolve these, the team created clear, step-by-step playbooks for different deal scenarios. They implemented a tiered approval matrix for discounts and non-standard terms.

But Olivia didn't stop there. Remembering the power of visualization, she had gigantic workflow diagrams printed and plastered on the office walls. She even created a life-sized board game in the breakroom, where team members could physically walk through the deal machine, rolling giant dice to simulate different scenarios.

The results? Well, let's just say they were more refreshing than a cold sip from a HydroSmarte bottle on a hot day.

Within a month, deal cycle times had decreased by 40 percent. Pricing consistency improved by 85 percent. The legal team started leaving the office before midnight. And customer satisfaction? It soared higher than a hang glider caught in an updraft.

But the real magic happened in an unexpected place. Remember those workflow diagrams on the walls? They became a gathering spot for spontaneous problem-solving sessions. Sales reps and finance analysts who had never spoken before suddenly huddled together, pointing at the diagrams and brainstorming ways to streamline the process even further.

Olivia stood back and watched with pride as her team took ownership of the process, constantly refining and improving it. She realized that by defining clear processes, she hadn't just created order out of chaos—she'd empowered her team to become process innovators themselves.

As she sipped from her HydroSmarte bottle (now with a new "Process Pro" limited edition design), Olivia smiled. She'd learned a valuable lesson: in the world of Deal Desks, well-defined processes aren't just about efficiency—they're about creating a culture of continuous improvement and collaboration.

So, the next time you find yourself drowning in deal chaos, remember Olivia and her HydroSmarte revolution. Take a deep breath, count down from five, and get ready to Marie Kondo your deal process. Who knows? You might just start a revolution of your own.

Olivia's experience at HydroSmarte demonstrates the impact of streamlined processes and workflows. Now, let's break down how you can achieve similar results in your Deal Desk.

THE BUILDING BLOCKS OF EFFECTIVE PROCESS DESIGN

Just like a ballet is made of various positions, steps, and movements, your Deal Desk processes are made of various tasks, decisions, and handoffs. The key to effective process design is to break down your end-to-end deal flow into its component parts, and then to define clear and consistent ways of executing each of those parts.

Use some of these key building blocks of effective Deal Desk process design:

1. Roles and responsibilities

   ⁓ One of the most critical elements of any process is the clear definition of who is responsible for what. In your Deal Desk processes, that means defining the specific roles and responsibilities of each team member, as well as any other stakeholders involved in the deal process.

   ⁓ Consider factors like decision-making authority, approval workflows, and communication protocols. The more clearly you can define who does what and when, the smoother and more efficient your deal process will be.

2. Input and output requirements

   ⁓ Another key element of process design is defining what information and materials are required at each stage of the process, and what outputs or deliverables are expected. This helps ensure everyone has what they need to do their job effectively, and that the process flows smoothly from one stage onto the next.

   ⁓ Consider factors like data and document requirements, quality standards, and timeline expectations. The more clearly you can define your input and output requirements, the less confusion and rework you'll encounter along the way.

3. Decision points and criteria

⟋ Every deal process involves decision points where choices will need to be made about how to proceed. Effective process design means defining clear criteria for how those decisions should be made, and who has the authority to make them.

⟋ Consider factors like pricing thresholds, risk assessment criteria, and escalation protocols. The more clearly you can define your decision points and criteria, the more consistent and objective your deal process will be.

4. Handoffs and transitions

⟋ Your deal process likely involves handoffs and transitions between different teams, systems, and stages. Effective process design means defining clear protocols for how those handoffs and transitions should happen, to ensure that nothing falls through the cracks.

⟋ Consider factors like notification and alert requirements, data and document transfer protocols, and service level agreements (SLAs). The more clearly you can define your handoffs and transitions, the less friction and delay you'll experience in your deal process.

DOCUMENTING AND COMMUNICATING YOUR PROCESSES

Once you've defined the building blocks of your Deal Desk processes, the next step is to document and communicate those processes to your team and stakeholders. This is where the choreography analogy really comes into play—just like a dancer needs a clear and detailed script to follow, your team needs a clear and detailed process document to guide their work.

Use some of these best practices for documenting and communicating your Deal Desk processes:

1. Use a consistent format and structure

    ◢ To make your process documentation easy to follow and understand, use a consistent format and structure across all your processes. This could include elements like process maps, swim lane diagrams, or step-by-step instructions.

    ◢ Consider factors like visual clarity, logical flow, and ease of reference. The more consistent and intuitive your process documentation is, the easier it will be for your team to reference, follow, and execute.

2. Include key details and context

   ⌐ Your process documentation should include all the key details and context needed to execute the process effectively. This could include information like roles and responsibilities, input and output requirements, decision criteria, and service level agreements.

   ⌐ Consider factors like level of detail, assumptions and dependencies, and links to related resources. The more comprehensive and self-contained your process documentation is, the less confusion and ambiguity your team will encounter.

3. Make it accessible and searchable

   ⌐ To be truly useful, your process documentation needs to be easily accessible and searchable by your team and stakeholders. This could mean storing it in a central repository, indexing it for search, or integrating it with your other tools and systems.

   ⌐ Consider factors like version control, access controls, and mobile compatibility. The more accessible and searchable your process documentation is, the more likely your team will use it and benefit from it.

4. Provide training and support

   ⟋ Documenting your processes is only half the battle—you also need to provide training and support to ensure that your team can execute those processes effectively. This could include elements like in-person training sessions, online tutorials, or ongoing coaching and feedback.

   ⟋ Consider factors like learning styles, skill levels, and performance metrics. The more training and support you provide around your processes, the more confident and capable your team will be in executing them.

CONTINUOUS IMPROVEMENT AND OPTIMIZATION

There is always room for refinement and improvement—your Deal Desk processes should never be considered set in stone. To truly achieve peak performance, you need to monitor, measure, and optimize your processes routinely over time.

Use these strategies for continuous improvement and optimization of your Deal Desk processes:

1. Establish performance metrics and KPIs

   ⟋ To know whether your processes are working effectively, you need to establish clear performance metrics and KPIs. These could include measures like cycle time, win rate, revenue impact, or customer satisfaction.

⟋ Consider factors like data quality, benchmarking, and alignment with business goals. The more relevant and actionable your performance metrics are, the more insight you'll have into where your processes are succeeding or falling short.

2. Conduct regular process audits and reviews

    ⟋ To identify opportunities for improvement, conduct regular audits and reviews of your Deal Desk processes. This could include elements like process walkthroughs, stakeholder interviews, or data analysis.

    ⟋ Consider factors like bottlenecks, error rates, and best practice deviations. The more rigorously and regularly you review your processes, the more opportunities you'll find to streamline and optimize them.

3. Implement incremental improvements

    ⟋ Based on your performance metrics and process reviews, implement incremental improvements to your Deal Desk processes. This could include elements like automating manual tasks, eliminating redundant steps, or adopting new best practices.

    ⟋ Consider factors like change management, user acceptance, and resource requirements. The more incrementally and iteratively you improve your processes, the less disruption and resistance you'll encounter along the way.

4. Foster a culture of continuous improvement

    ⁄ To truly achieve peak performance, you need to foster a culture of continuous improvement within your Deal Desk team. This means encouraging experimentation, risk-taking, and learning from failure. Reward team members who drive process innovation and optimization.

    ⁄ Consider factors like recognition programs, innovation challenges, and cross-functional collaboration. The more you can embed continuous improvement into the DNA of your Deal Desk culture, the more sustainable and impactful your process optimizations will be.

Developing effective Deal Desk processes can be complex, especially for organizations new to structured deal management. Deal Solutions offers process development services, helping businesses create tailored, efficient workflows that align with their unique needs and goals.

ENCORE! BRINGING YOUR DEAL DESK PROCESSES TO LIFE

Bravo, director—you have a leader or a team who has defined, documented, and optimized your Deal Desk processes to perfection. They've created clear and compelling choreography for the dance of the deal and equipped your team with the scripts and skills they need to execute it flawlessly.

But remember—the true test of your process design isn't in the documentation or the diagrams but in the actual performance of your team. Just like a ballet comes to life on the stage, your Deal Desk processes come to life in the day-to-day work of your team as they collaborate, communicate, and problem-solve their way through each deal.

As you watch your team perform, keep an eye out for opportunities to refine and improve your processes even further. Maybe there's a new technology or tool that could streamline a particular step or a new best practice that could increase win rates or customer satisfaction. Maybe there's a rising star on your team who has ideas for how to take your processes to the next level or a customer insight that could inform an alternative approach to deal-making.

Whatever opportunities you identify, don't be afraid to iterate and experiment. The most successful Deal Desks are the ones that are constantly pushing the boundaries of what's possible and always striving to deliver more value and impact to the business.

So, take a bow, director—you've created a masterpiece of Deal Desk process design. But don't rest on your laurels just yet. The dance of the deal is forever developing, and there's always room for one more encore. Keep choreographing, optimizing, and striving for peak performance, and you'll be sure to earn a standing ovation from your customers, stakeholders, and team.

CHAPTER 8

EFFECTIVE COMMUNICATION AND COLLABORATION

Cut to the chase! Your Deal Desk is ready to take center stage with a star-studded cast, a cutting-edge set, and a script honed to perfection. But as any director knows, even the best-laid plans can go awry if the actors aren't in sync, the crew isn't on the same page, or communication breaks down.

Before we dive into the nitty-gritty of communication and collaboration within the Deal Desk, let's take a moment to address the elephant in the room. Some of what I'm about to discuss might seem like People Management 101. You might be thinking, "I've heard this all before," or, "My team already has this down pat."

If that is the case, fantastic! Feel free to skim this chapter or skip ahead. You're already ahead of the game, and your future

Deal Desk will likely reap the benefits of your stellar culture and finely-honed soft skills.

However, I'd be remiss if I didn't emphasize the critical importance of these "basics." In my twenty-plus years of experience, I've seen countless companies—from scrappy startups to Fortune 500 giants—stumble not because of technical shortcomings but due to breakdowns in communication, collaboration, and culture.

Hiring the right leaders and fostering the right culture can make or break a company, particularly in the high-stakes, fast-paced Deal Desk world. Let's explore how effective communication and collaboration can transform your Deal Desk from a group of individuals into a cohesive, high-performing team that drives real business impact.

And remember, within a Deal Desk, your people and your culture aren't just nice-to-haves: they're your secret weapons for success. Now, let's dive in!

Effective communication and collaboration are the lifeblood of a successful Deal Desk. When team members communicate clearly and work together seamlessly, they can overcome any challenge and achieve remarkable results.

Alone, we can do so little; together, we can do so much.

— *Helen Keller*

In the Deal Desk, it's not just about exchanging information; it's about building relationships, fostering trust, and working toward common goals. By prioritizing clear communication and collaborative practices, you create an environment where ideas flow freely, problems are solved efficiently, and everyone is empowered to contribute their best.

To do that, you need to look at the key principles and practices that underpin successful teamwork, the common pitfalls and challenges that can derail it, and the strategies and tools you can use to keep everyone on the same page and moving in the same direction. Once you do, you'll have a clear roadmap for building a Deal Desk culture that's not just high performing, but truly collaborative and communicative.

THE PRINCIPLES OF EFFECTIVE DEAL DESK COMMUNICATION

Just like any great film or play, effective Deal Desk communication starts with a set of core principles that guide everything else. These principles are the foundation upon which you should build all your communication strategies and tactics, and they apply whether you're communicating with your team, other departments, or external stakeholders.

The key principles of effective Deal Desk communication are:

1. Clarity and conciseness

    ⟩ In the fast-paced world of Deal Desks, there's no time for ambiguity or confusion. Your communication should be clear, concise, and to the point, whether you're writing an email, giving a presentation, or having a one-on-one conversation.

⟋ Use simple, jargon-free language, and focus on the key points and action items. If you can say it in ten words instead of twenty, do it. Your team will thank you for it.

2. Timeliness and relevance

⟋ Effective communication is not just about what you say but when you say it. In a Deal Desk context, timeliness is everything—you need to communicate the right information to the right people at the right time, or you risk missing critical deadlines or decisions.

⟋ Make sure your communication is always relevant and timely, and use tools like email alerts, notifications, and project management software to keep everyone on track and up to date.

3. Transparency and openness

⟋ Trust is the glue that holds any high-performing team together; transparency is the key to building that trust. In your Deal Desk communication, strive to be as open and transparent as possible about your goals, challenges, successes, and failures.

⟋ Encourage your team to do the same and create a culture where it's safe to ask questions, raise concerns, and make mistakes. The more transparent and open your communication is, the more trust and collaboration you'll foster.

4. Empathy and understanding

    ⟩ At the end of the day, your Deal Desk is made up
    of people—people with different backgrounds,
    perspectives, and communication styles. To
    communicate effectively, you need to put yourself
    in their shoes and understand where they're
    coming from.

    ⟩ Practice active listening, ask questions, and seek
    to understand before seeking to be understood.
    The more empathy and understanding you bring
    to your communication, the more effective and
    resonant it will be.

THE PRACTICES OF EFFECTIVE DEAL DESK COLLABORATION

Of course, principles are just the starting point—to truly
achieve effective Deal Desk communication and collaboration,
you need to put those principles into practice. And that means
building a set of collaboration practices embedded into your
team's DNA, processes, and culture.

Some of the key practices of effective Deal Desk collaboration are:

1. Regular check-ins and status updates

    › One of the most important practices of effective collaboration is regular communication—not just about the big things, but about the small things, too. Ensure your team has regular check-ins and status updates, whether it's a daily standup meeting, a weekly progress report, or a monthly all-hands.

    › Use these check-ins to share updates, identify roadblocks, and ensure everyone is on track and in alignment. The more frequently and consistently you communicate, the more in sync and collaborative your team will be.

2. Clear roles and responsibilities

    › Another key practice of effective collaboration is the clear definition of roles and responsibilities. Everyone on your Deal Desk team should know exactly what they're responsible for, what's expected of them, and how their work fits into the bigger picture.

    › Use tools like RACI (Responsible, Accountable, Consulted, and Informed) matrices, job descriptions, and project plans to define and communicate roles and responsibilities. The more clarity and transparency you have around who does what, the less confusion and duplication of effort you'll have.

3. Collaborative tools and technologies

   ⟩ In today's fast-paced, distributed work environment, collaboration tools and technologies keep everyone connected and aligned. From project management software to instant messaging to video conferencing, countless tools are available to help your team collaborate more effectively.

   ⟩ Choose tools that are easy to use, integrate well with your existing systems and processes, and support your team's unique collaboration needs. Ensure everyone on your team is trained and comfortable using them—the best tools in the world won't help if no one knows how to use them.

4. Continuous feedback and improvement

   ⟩ Finally, effective collaboration is not a one-time event—it's an ongoing process of feedback, learning, and improvement. Make sure your team has regular opportunities to give and receive feedback, both on their individual work and on the team's collaboration as a whole. Creating a culture of open feedback is one of the best things you can do for the long-term success of the organization.

Use retrospectives, surveys, and other feedback mechanisms to identify areas for improvement and make a plan to address them. The more consistently and proactively you seek to improve your collaboration, the more effective and impactful it will be.

OVERCOMING COMMON COLLABORATION CHALLENGES

Of course, even with the best principles and practices in place, collaboration is never easy. Challenges and obstacles often get in the way, from conflicting priorities to communication breakdowns to personality clashes.

Unresolved conflict and combative personalities on a team can be incredibly debilitating. It is always best to nip these instances in the bud. Do not be afraid to adjust the team accordingly when someone does not fit in with a positive and transformational culture.

Here are some of the most common collaboration challenges that Deal Desks face and some strategies for overcoming them:

1. Silos and disconnects

    One of the biggest challenges of Deal Desk collaboration is breaking down the silos and disconnects that can exist between different departments, functional areas, and stakeholders. When everyone is working in their own bubble, it's easy for communication to break down and for important information to fall through the cracks.

, To overcome this challenge, build cross-functional relationships and communication channels. Encourage your team to reach out proactively to other departments, share information and insights, and work together to solve problems. The more you can break down the barriers between teams, the more collaborative and effective your Deal Desk will be.

2. Conflicting priorities and goals

, Another common collaboration challenge is conflicting priorities and goals. When different stakeholders have different objectives and incentives, it's hard to find common ground and make decisions everyone can get behind.

, To overcome this challenge, focus on finding win-win solutions that balance the needs and goals of all stakeholders. Use tools like decision matrices and weighted scoring to evaluate options objectively and find the best path forward. And make sure everyone understands the reasoning behind the decision, even if they don't agree with it 100 percent.

3. Lack of accountability and follow-through

> A third collaboration challenge that many Deal Desks face is lack of accountability and follow-through. When everyone is responsible for everything, it's easy for things to fall through the cracks and important tasks to go uncompleted.

> To overcome this challenge, focus on creating clear accountability structures and follow-up processes. Use tools like action trackers and project management software to assign tasks, set deadlines, and track progress. And make sure everyone knows what's expected of them and what the consequences are for not following through.

4. Personality conflicts and communication breakdowns

> Finally, one of the most difficult types of collaboration challenges to overcome is personality conflicts and communication breakdowns. When team members have different communication styles, work preferences, or interpersonal dynamics, it can be hard to work together effectively.

> To overcome this challenge, focus on building a culture of empathy, respect, and open communication. Encourage your team to seek to understand each other's perspectives and needs, and to find ways to work together that play to everyone's strengths. And when conflicts

arise, address them head-on with a spirit of collaboration and problem-solving rather than with blame or defensiveness.

THE ROLE OF LEADERSHIP IN DEAL DESK COLLABORATION

Of course, no discussion of Deal Desk collaboration would be complete without talking about the role of leadership. The director of your Deal Desk plays a critical role in setting the tone, modeling the behavior, and creating the conditions for effective collaboration to thrive. If you are the leader of your startup, you're ultimately accountable for ensuring your Deal Desk is in a position to succeed.

Here are some critical ways that you can lead your Deal Desk to collaborative success:

1. Set a clear vision and strategy

   ⸍ It's up to you to set a clear vision and strategy for what you want to achieve and how you want to achieve it. Make sure your team understands the bigger picture and how their individual work fits into it.

   ⸍ Communicate your vision and strategy clearly and consistently, and ensure the team is aligned around it. The more clarity and direction you can provide, the more focused and collaborative your team will be.

2. Model collaborative behavior

⟋ As a leader, your actions speak louder than your words. If you want your team to collaborate effectively, you need to model that behavior yourself. That means being open, transparent, and inclusive in your communication and actively seeking opportunities to work with others.

⟋ It also means being willing to listen to feedback, admit mistakes, and change course when needed. The more you can model a collaborative mindset and approach, the more your team will follow suit.

3. Foster a culture of trust and psychological safety

⟋ Effective collaboration depends on trust—in each other, the process, and leadership. As a leader, it's up to you to foster a culture of trust and psychological safety where everyone feels comfortable speaking up, taking risks, and being vulnerable.

⟋ That means creating a safe space for open communication, encouraging healthy conflict and debate, and rewarding honesty and transparency. It also means responding to feedback and concerns and taking action to address them. The more trust and safety you can create, the more collaborative and innovative your team will be.

4. Provide the resources and support needed for success

⟋ Finally, as a leader, it's your job to make sure your team has the resources and support they need to collaborate effectively. That means providing the right tools and technologies, the right training and development opportunities, and the right recognition and rewards.

It also means advocating for your team and removing any barriers or roadblocks impeding their success. The more you can support and empower your team, the more they'll be able to achieve together.

TAKE A BOW: THE POWER OF EFFECTIVE COMMUNICATION AND COLLABORATION

You've learned the principles and practices of effective Deal Desk communication and collaboration, the common challenges and how to overcome them, and the critical role that leadership plays in fostering a collaborative culture.

But remember—just like a great film or play, effective collaboration is not a one-time event, but an ongoing process of learning, adapting, and improving. It takes constant effort, attention, and commitment from everyone involved—from the director to the cast to the crew.

So, as you leave this chapter and head back to your own Deal Desk stage, keep these lessons in mind: communicate clearly and concisely, be transparent and open, and always strive for empathy and understanding. Build a set of collaboration practices that work for your team, and continuously seek feedback and improvement. As a leader, set the vision, model the behavior, foster the trust, and provide the support that your team needs to succeed.

If you can do all that, you'll be well on your way to creating a Deal Desk that's not just high-performing but truly collaborative and communicative. A Deal Desk where everyone works together seamlessly, no matter what challenges arise. A Deal Desk that's ready to take center stage and steal the show.

So, take a bow, director—you've earned it. And remember— the secret sauce of Deal Desk success is not just in the script, the set, or the cast, but in the way you all work together to bring it to life. Here's to many more successful collaborations, and many more standing ovations.

CHAPTER 9

METRICS AND MEASUREMENT

Your Deal Desk is smoothly running, with a star-studded cast, a streamlined script, and a collaborative culture that's the envy of the business world. But as any good director knows, it's not enough to just put on a great show—you also need to know how well it's performing and what you can do to make it even better.

That's where metrics and measurement come in. Just like box office numbers and critical reviews tell the story of a film's success, Deal Desk metrics and measurement tell the story of your team's performance—what's working, what's not, and where there's room for improvement.

The first guy through the wall
always gets bloody. Always.

—*Moneyball*

Just as I had to measure and adjust every angle of entry when diving into that tiny pool, implementing a robust system for tracking and analyzing performance metrics can be challenging, but it's essential for long-term success. By measuring the right KPIs, you can identify areas for improvement, optimize processes, and ensure that your Deal Desk is contributing to the organization's overall objectives.

But with so many aspects of Deal Desk performance to track—from deal velocity to win rates to compliance and more—it is overwhelming to know where to start, and how to make sense of all the data. That's why it's time to break down the deal machine metrics and measurement and give you a clear roadmap for keeping score of your team's success.

We'll start by exploring the key metrics that every Deal Desk should track, and why they matter. Then we'll dive into the tools and techniques for collecting, analyzing, and visualizing that data in a way that's actionable and impactful. And finally, we'll discuss how to use your metrics and measurement to drive continuous improvement and optimization and take your Deal Desk performance to the next level.

Grab your popcorn and get ready to crunch some numbers—it's time to bring your Deal Desk metrics to life on the big screen.

THE KEY METRICS EVERY DEAL DESK SHOULD TRACK

When it comes to Deal Desk metrics, there's no shortage of data points you could be tracking. But not all metrics are created equal—some are more critical than others for understanding and improving your team's performance.

Here are some of the key performance indicators that every Deal Desk should know about their business:

1. Deal Velocity

    , Definition: The average time it takes for a deal to move through your pipeline, from initial contact to closed-won.

    , Why it matters: Deal velocity is a key indicator of the efficiency and effectiveness of your deal process. The faster you can move deals through the pipeline, the more revenue you can generate and the better experience you can provide for your customers.

2. Win Rate

    , Definition: The percentage of deals that you close-win out of all the deals in your pipeline.

    , Why it matters: Win rate is a key indicator of the quality and competitiveness of your deals. The higher your win rate, the more effective your team is at qualifying, pursuing, and closing the right opportunities.

3. Average Deal Size

    , Definition: The average revenue or value of your closed-won deals.

, Why it matters: Average deal size is a key indicator of the impact and profitability of your deals. The larger your average deal size, the more revenue you can generate with fewer resources and the more strategic value you can provide to your business.

4. Pricing Accuracy

, Definition: The percentage of deals priced correctly and consistently according to your pricing guidelines and approval matrix.

, Why it matters: Pricing accuracy is a key indicator of the compliance and control of your deal process. The more accurate your pricing is, the less risk you have of leaving money on the table or creating downstream billing and revenue recognition issues.

5. Contract Cycle Time

, Definition: The average time to draft, negotiate, and execute a contract once a deal has been approved.

, Why it matters: Contract cycle time is a key indicator of the speed and efficiency of your legal and contract management process. The faster you can get contracts signed, the faster you can recognize revenue, and the better experience you can provide for your customers.

6. Customer Satisfaction

- Definition: The percentage of customers who are satisfied or very satisfied with their experience working with your Deal Desk.

- Why it matters: Customer satisfaction is a key indicator of the quality and value of your Deal Desk services. The more satisfied your customers are, the more likely they are to renew, expand, and advocate for your business.

Of course, these are just a few examples. The specific metrics that matter most for your Deal Desk will depend on your unique goals, challenges, and stakeholders. By focusing on a core set of metrics that align with your strategic priorities, you can create a clear and convincing scorecard for your Deal Desk performance.

COLLECTING, ANALYZING, AND VISUALIZING YOUR DEAL DESK DATA

Of course, tracking your Deal Desk metrics is just the first step—to really understand and act on that data, you need to collect, analyze, and visualize it in a way that's meaningful and actionable.

Use these tips and best practices for making the most of your Deal Desk data:

1. Centralize your data sources

   - One of the biggest challenges of Deal Desk metrics is that the data often lives in multiple systems and tools—from your CRM to your CPQ to your contract management system and more. To get a complete and accurate picture of your performance, you need to be able to centralize and integrate that data into a single source of truth, as we discussed more in-depth in Chapter 6.

⟋ Look for tools and platforms that can help you connect and harmonize your data across systems and create a unified view of your Deal Desk metrics. This could be a dedicated business intelligence tool, a custom dashboard or report, or even a simple spreadsheet that brings together data from multiple sources.

2. Establish clear definitions, standards, and data governance

⟋ Another challenge of Deal Desk metrics is that different people and teams may have different definitions and interpretations of what each metric means and how to calculate it. To ensure consistency and accuracy in your data, you need to establish clear definitions and standards for each metric.

⟋ Work with your key stakeholders to agree on a common language and methodology for your metrics, and document those standards in a central repository that everyone can access and reference. Make sure to train your team on those standards and hold them accountable for adhering to them in their data entry and reporting.

3. Use data visualization to tell a story

    ›   Numbers and spreadsheets can be dry and overwhelming, especially for non-technical stakeholders. To make your Deal Desk data come alive and drive action, you need to visualize it in a way that's engaging and intuitive.

    ›   Use data visualization tools and techniques—like charts, graphs, dashboards, and infographics—to create an apparent and absorbing narrative around your metrics. Highlight the key insights and trends, making it easy for people to understand what the data is saying and what they should do about it.

4. Make it actionable and value accountability

    ›   Metrics and measurement are only valuable if they lead to action and improvement. To make your Deal Desk data truly impactful, you need to connect it to specific actions and accountability.

    ›   For each metric, identify the key drivers and levers that impact it, and create a plan for how you will move the needle. Assign clear ownership and responsibility for each metric and hold your team accountable for delivering results. Regularly review and discuss your metrics with your stakeholders and work with them to inform your strategic decisions and priorities.

By following these tips and best practices, you can turn your Deal Desk data into a powerful asset that drives performance and growth. But it's not just about the data itself—it's also about the culture and mindset you create around it.

CREATING A CULTURE OF DATA-DRIVEN DECISION-MAKING

Metrics and measurement are only as valuable as the culture and mindset surrounding them. If your team sees data as a burden or a box to check rather than a tool for learning and improvement, then even the most sophisticated metrics and dashboards will fall flat.

That's why creating a culture of data-driven decision-making is so critical for Deal Desk success. Use these key principles and practices for fostering that culture:

1. Make data a core value

   ⟩ To create a culture of data-driven decision-making, you need to make data a core value of your Deal Desk. That means explicitly prioritizing and celebrating the use of data in your team's work and making it a key part of your team's identity and purpose.

   ⟩ Communicate the importance of data early and often—make it a regular part of your team's conversations and rituals. Recognize and reward team members who excel at using data to drive insights and action and clarify that data is not just a nice-to-have but a must-have for success.

2. Empower your team with data literacy

⟋ To make data-driven decisions, your team needs to be data literate—that is, they need to have the skills and knowledge to understand, interpret, and act on data. But data literacy is not a given—it's a skill that needs to be developed and nurtured.

⟋ Invest in training and development programs that help your team build their data literacy, from basic data concepts and terminology to more advanced analytics and visualization techniques. Create opportunities for your team to practice and apply those skills in real-world situations, with guidance and feedback from more experienced data practitioners.

3. Make data accessible and transparent

⟋ Data-driven decision-making depends on having access to the right data at the right time. But too often, data is siloed, gated, or hidden away in complex systems and tools that only a few experts can navigate.

⟋ To create a culture of data-driven decision-making, you need to make data accessible and transparent to everyone on your team. That means creating user-friendly dashboards, reports, and tools that make it easy for people to find and explore the data they need and providing clear documentation and support to help them understand and use that data effectively.

4. Encourage experimentation and learning

> Data-driven decision-making is not about having all the answers—it's about asking the right questions and using data to test and learn from different approaches and hypotheses. To create a culture of data-driven decision-making, you need to encourage experimentation and learning, even if it means sometimes getting things wrong.

> Create a safe and supportive environment for your team to try new things, take risks, and learn from their mistakes. Celebrate the process of experimentation and iteration, not just the results, and clarify that failure is not a problem as long as it leads to learning and improvement.

By following these principles and practices, you can create a culture of data-driven decision-making that empowers your team to use metrics and measurement to drive real impact and value for your Deal Desk and your business. But it's not a one-time effort—it's an ongoing journey of learning, adapting, and improving, just like the metrics themselves.

METRICS IN ACTION: A DEAL DESK EXAMPLE

To bring this all to life, let's look at an example of how one company used metrics and measurement to transform its Deal Desk performance.

Acme Inc. was a fast-growing software company that had recently implemented a Deal Desk to manage its complex sales processes and pricing scenarios. However, after a few months of operation, the Deal Desk was struggling to keep up with the volume and velocity of deals, and there were growing concerns about the accuracy and consistency of their pricing and approvals.

To address these challenges, the Deal Desk team decided to implement a metrics and measurement program to track and improve their performance. They started by identifying a core set of metrics that aligned with their key goals and challenges, including:

- Deal velocity: The average time from deal creation to approval

- Pricing accuracy: The percentage of deals that were priced correctly according to their guidelines

- Approval rate: The percentage of deals that were approved by the Deal Desk on the first submission

- Customer satisfaction: The net promoter score (NPS) of customers who went through the Deal Desk process

They then worked with their IT and operations teams to centralize and integrate the data needed to calculate these metrics using a combination of their CRM, CPQ, and billing systems. They also established clear definitions and standards for each metric and trained their team on how to interpret and act on the data.

Next, they created a set of dashboards and reports to visualize and communicate their metrics to key stakeholders across the business. They used a mix of charts, graphs, and tables to highlight the key trends and insights and provided simple explanations and recommendations for what the data meant and what actions should be taken.

Finally, they implemented a regular cadence of review meetings and discussions around their metrics, with weekly check-ins for the Deal Desk team and monthly business reviews with executive leadership. They used these forums to celebrate successes, identify areas for improvement, and align on strategic priorities and initiatives.

The results were impressive. Within the first quarter of implementing their metrics program, Acme's Deal Desk saw:

- A 25 percent reduction in average deal velocity, from twenty days to fifteen days

- A 15 percent improvement in pricing accuracy, from 80 percent to 92 percent

- A 20 percent increase in approval rate, from 60 percent to 72 percent

- A 10-point increase in customer NPS, from 30 to 40

Perhaps more importantly, the metrics program helped to create a culture of data-driven decision-making and continuous improvement within the Deal Desk team. They became more proactive and strategic in their approach, using data to identify opportunities and challenges and test and learn from different approaches and solutions.

And as the Deal Desk team's performance improved, so did their reputation and impact across the business. They became seen as a strategic partner and driver of value rather than just a back-office function. They could also secure additional resources and investment to continue scaling and optimizing their operations.

Of course, this is just one example, and every company's Deal Desk metrics journey will vary. However, the key principles and practices remain the same: identify the metrics that matter, make the data accessible and actionable, and foster a culture of data-driven decision-making and continuous improvement.

MEASURING UP: THE FUTURE OF DEAL DESK METRICS

As we've seen throughout this chapter, metrics and measurement are essential for driving Deal Desk performance and growth. But the world of metrics is always evolving, and what works today may not work tomorrow.

As you continue on your own Deal Desk metrics journey, keep some of these trends and opportunities in mind:

1. The rise of predictive and prescriptive analytics

   ⟩ Today, most Deal Desk metrics are descriptive—they tell you what happened in the past. But the future of metrics is predictive and prescriptive—using advanced analytics and AI to forecast what will happen in the future and to recommend the best actions to take.

   ⟩ As Deal Desks generate more data, there will be increasing opportunities to use that data to build predictive models and algorithms that can help you optimize your pricing, prioritize your pipeline, and anticipate customer needs and behaviors. As those models become more sophisticated, they will be able to not just predict outcomes, but prescribe the specific actions and decisions that will drive the best results.

2. The importance of real-time, self-service metrics and data governance

   ⟩ In the fast-paced world of sales and deals, metrics that are even a day old can be obsolete. That's why the future of Deal Desk metrics is real-time and self-service—providing instant access to the latest data and insights, and empowering teams to explore and act on that data on their own.

   ⟩ This will require a shift away from static reports and dashboards, and toward more dynamic and interactive tools that can update and adapt in real-time. It will also require a greater focus on data governance and quality, to ensure that the data being used is accurate, consistent, and trustworthy.

3. The emergence of new and novel metrics

, As Deal Desks evolve and mature, so too will the metrics they use to measure their performance. Besides the traditional metrics like velocity and win rate, we may see the emergence of novel metrics that capture the unique value and impact of Deal Desks.

, For example, we may see metrics around deal complexity, risk management, or customer lifetime value that help to quantify the strategic role that Deal Desks play in driving long-term business success. We may also see metrics that capture the softer aspects of Deal Desk performance—like collaboration, innovation, and employee engagement—that are critical for building high-performing teams.

The key is to stay curious and keep exploring and experimenting with new metrics and measurement approaches. The most successful Deal Desks will be the ones that are always looking for new and better ways to understand and improve their performance and drive value for their customers and their business.

CONCLUSION

Metrics and measurement may not be the most glamorous part of running a Deal Desk, but they are essential for success. By tracking the right metrics, analyzing the right data, and creating the right culture, you can turn your Deal Desk into a data-driven powerhouse that consistently delivers results.

But it's not just about the numbers—it's about the insights, the actions, and the impact that those numbers enable. When you use metrics and measurement to tell a compelling story about your Deal Desk's performance and to drive meaningful change and improvement, that's when the real magic happens.

As you continue on your own Deal Desk journey, remember to keep score, keep learning, and keep pushing the boundaries of what's possible. With the right metrics and measurements in place, there's no limit to how far your Deal Desk can go.

And who knows—maybe one day your Deal Desk's metrics will be the stuff of legend, inspiring future generations of dealmakers and data-driven leaders. But even if they don't make it to the big screen, they will still be the key to your Deal Desk's success, and the foundation for a future of growth, innovation, and impact.

So, roll out the red carpet, strike up the band, and let the metrics show begin!

PART 4

SCALING YOUR DEAL DESK

CHAPTER 10

ADAPTING TO GROWTH

In this chapter, we'll explore the key challenges of Deal Desk growth, strategies for adaptation, and real-world examples of successful scaling.

The camera fades in on a bustling office, where the once-intimate Deal Desk team has grown into a thriving, multi-faceted deal machine. The cast of characters has expanded, the script has become more complex, and the stakes have never been higher. Welcome to the world of Deal Desk growth— where adaptation is the name of the game, and the ability to scale seamlessly is the key to box office success.

In the early days of your Deal Desk journey, things were simpler. You had a tight-knit team, a straightforward process, and a manageable volume of deals to oversee. But as your business has grown, so too have the demands on your Deal Desk. Suddenly, you're dealing with a larger and more diverse customer base, a more complex product portfolio, and a dizzying array of new challenges and opportunities.

It's a classic plot twist in the Deal Desk story—the moment when the scrappy underdog becomes the big-league player and must adapt to a whole new level of complexity and scale. And just like any good movie hero, your Deal Desk must rise to the occasion and find new ways to thrive in the face of change.

To do that, your Deal Desk must grow and adapt. We'll delve into the key challenges and opportunities that come with scaling your operation and provide a roadmap for navigating the twists and turns of Deal Desk expansion. Along the way, we'll share examples and best practices from Deal Desks that have successfully made the leap to the big time and come out stronger on the other side.

So, grab your popcorn and get ready for the next act in your Deal Desk journey. It's time to embrace the chaos and adapt your way to major success.

THE CHALLENGES OF DEAL DESK GROWTH

Before we dive into strategies for adapting to Deal Desk growth, let's take a closer look at the key challenges that come with scaling an operation. These obstacles and roadblocks can trip up even the most well-oiled Deal Desk machine, and understanding them is the first step to overcoming them.

1. Increasing volume and complexity of deals

   / As your business grows, so does the volume and complexity of the deals that your Deal Desk must manage. You may deal with a broader range of products, pricing models, and customer segments, each with unique requirements and challenges.

   / This increasing complexity can strain your existing processes, technology, and systems and make it harder to maintain the same level of speed, accuracy, and consistency that you had in the early days. It can also lead to bottlenecks and delays as your team struggles to keep up with the sheer volume of deals flowing through the pipeline.

2. Expanding and diversifying customer base

   / Another key challenge of Deal Desk growth is the expanding and diversifying customer base that comes with it. As you move upmarket or enter new industries and geographies, you may encounter a whole new set of customer needs, preferences, and expectations.

   / This can require significant changes to your Deal Desk strategy and approach as you adapt to new buyer personas, decision-making processes, and cultural norms. It can also require new skills and expertise within your team as you navigate the nuances of different customer segments and markets.

3. Evolving product and pricing strategy

 As your business grows and develops, so too does your product and pricing strategy. You may introduce new offerings, bundles, and pricing tiers or experiment with new go-to-market approaches and sales motions.

 This constant state of change can be both exciting and challenging for your Deal Desk as you work to stay aligned with the latest product and pricing developments and ensure that your processes and policies keep pace. It can also require a greater degree of collaboration and communication with other teams—such as product management, marketing, and sales—than ever before.

4. Growing and changing the Deal Desk team

 Perhaps the most significant challenge of Deal Desk growth is the growing and changing Deal Desk team itself. As your operation scales, you may need to add new roles and responsibilities, restructure your team, and bring on new talent to support the increasing volume and complexity of your deals.

 This can be a delicate balancing act as you work to maintain the culture, collaboration, and consistency which have made your Deal Desk successful thus far while also adapting to the needs of a larger and more diverse team. It can also require significant investment in training, development, and change management to ensure that your team is equipped to handle the new challenges and opportunities that come with growth.

These are just a few of the many challenges that can come with Deal Desk growth—and navigating them successfully requires a combination of strategic planning, operational excellence, and sheer determination. But for those Deal Desks that can adapt and thrive in the face of these challenges, the rewards can be significant—from increased revenue and market share to improved customer satisfaction and team morale. Now that we've identified the key challenges, let's explore how to evolve your tech stack to meet these growing demands.

EVOLVING YOUR TECH STACK: SCALING YOUR DEAL DESK TOOLS FOR GROWTH

As your startup scales and your Deal Desk matures, you'll likely find that the technology solutions that served you well in the early days may no longer be sufficient. This isn't a setback—it's a sign of success! Your growing needs reflect your company's expansion and the increasing sophistication of your deal processes.

While Chapter 6 focused on establishing your initial tech stack, this section is about leveling up. It's time to celebrate your success and reinvest in your Deal Desk's capabilities. Here's what to consider as you evolve your technology:

1. Scalability and Performance: Your original tools may struggle with increased deal volume. Look for enterprise-grade solutions that can handle many concurrent users and transactions without compromising speed or reliability.

2. Advanced Analytics and AI Capabilities: With more data at your disposal, seek out tools that offer sophisticated analytics and AI features. These can provide deeper insights, predictive modeling, and automation of complex tasks.

3. Customization and Flexibility: As your processes become more refined, you'll need tools that allow for greater customization. Look for platforms with robust APIs and extensibility options that can be tailored to your specific workflows.

4. Integration Capabilities: Your tech stack should now seamlessly integrate with a wider array of systems, from advanced CRM platforms to ERP systems to business intelligence tools. Prioritize solutions that offer pre-built connectors or open architectures for easy integration.

5. Compliance and Security Features: With growth comes increased scrutiny. Ensure your new tools meet stringent security standards and offer features

to support regulatory compliance such as advanced encryption, audit trails, and role-based access controls.

6. Global Capabilities: If international expansion is on the horizon, look for tools that support multiple currencies, languages, and region-specific compliance requirements.

7. Collaboration Features: As your team grows, you'll need more robust collaboration tools. Look for features like real-time co-editing, advanced commenting systems, and integrated communication platforms.

8. Mobile Accessibility: With deals happening around the clock and around the globe, mobile access is no longer a nice-to-have. Prioritize tools with full-featured mobile apps or responsive web interfaces.

Remember, upgrading your tech stack isn't just about keeping up with your growth—it's about accelerating it. These more advanced tools can unlock new efficiencies, provide deeper insights, and empower your Deal Desk to take on more strategic roles within the organization.

As you evaluate new technologies, involve your Deal Desk team in the process. They'll have valuable insights into what features would most impact their daily work. Also, consider engaging with peers at other high-growth companies to learn from their experiences.

Investing in more sophisticated tools is a tangible way to recognize your Deal Desk's contributions to your company's success. It sends a clear message that you're committed to supporting their work and positioning them for even more significant impact in the future.

By continuously evolving your tech stack, you ensure that your Deal Desk remains a cutting-edge function capable of supporting your company's ambitious growth targets and maintaining your competitive edge in the market. With your tech stack optimized for growth, let's turn our attention to strategies for adapting your Deal Desk operations as a whole.

STRATEGIES FOR ADAPTING TO DEAL DESK GROWTH

So how can your Deal Desk adapt to the challenges of growth and emerge stronger and more successful on the other side? Drawing from the challenges we identified earlier, here are key strategies to help your Deal Desk adapt and thrive:

1. Streamline and automate processes

    , One of the most effective ways to adapt to Deal Desk growth is to streamline and automate your processes wherever possible. This can help you manage increasing volume and complexity while also freeing up your team to focus on higher-value activities.

    , Look for opportunities to standardize and templatize your deal structures, pricing models, and approval workflows, and invest in tools and technologies that can automate manual tasks and decision-making. As you evolve your tech stack, ensure that you're integrating it into the right operational functions.

2. Invest in data and analytics

   - Another key strategy for adapting to Deal Desk growth is to invest in data and analytics capabilities. As your operation scales, the ability to track, measure, and analyze your deal performance becomes increasingly critical.

   - Build out robust data infrastructure and reporting tools that can give you real-time visibility into key metrics like deal velocity, win rates, and revenue impact. Use this data to identify trends, patterns, and opportunities for optimization, and to make data-driven decisions about where to focus your resources and efforts.

3. Foster a culture of continuous learning and improvement

   - Adapting to Deal Desk growth is not a one-time event, but an ongoing process of learning, experimentation, and improvement. To stay ahead of the curve, it's important to foster a culture of continuous learning and development within your team.

   - Encourage your team members to seek new skills and knowledge, and provide them with the training, coaching, and resources they need to grow and adapt. Create forums and channels for sharing best practices, lessons learned, and innovative ideas across the team, and celebrate the successes and failures that come with trying new things.

4. Collaborate and align with other teams

⁄ As your Deal Desk grows, it becomes increasingly important to collaborate and align with other teams across the organization. From sales and marketing to product and finance, the success of your Deal Desk depends on your ability to work seamlessly with a wide range of stakeholders.

⁄ Invest in building strong relationships and communication channels with these teams, and seek opportunities to align your goals, metrics, and processes. Look for ways to use their expertise and insights to inform your own strategy and decision-making and to create a more cohesive and integrated go-to-market approach.

5. Stay customer-centric

⁄ Finally, one of the most important strategies for adapting to Deal Desk growth is to stay laser-focused on your customers. As your business evolves and expands, it's easy to lose sight of the needs and preferences of the customers you serve.

⁄ Keep your customers at the center of everything you do, and use their feedback and insights to guide your Deal Desk strategy and operations. Regularly solicit input and feedback from your customers and use it to identify areas for improvement and innovation. Always be willing to adapt and pivot your approach based on what you learn in order to deliver the best possible experience and outcomes for your customers.

These strategies directly address the challenges we discussed earlier. Let's see how they play out in real-world scenarios. By implementing these strategies and best practices, your Deal Desk can not only adapt to the challenges of growth but thrive in the face of them. You'll be able to scale your operation with confidence, knowing that you have the processes, tools, and mindset in place to handle whatever plot twists and turns come your way.

ILLUSTRATIVE EXAMPLES OF DEAL DESK GROWTH AND ADAPTATION

To bring these strategies to life, let's look at a few examples of Deal Desks that have successfully navigated the challenges of growth and adaptation. The following examples demonstrate how companies have successfully implemented the strategies we've discussed:

1. Acme Inc.

   , Acme Inc. is a fast-growing enterprise software company that has seen its Deal Desk explode in size and complexity over the past few years. To adapt to this growth, the company has invested heavily in automation and data analytics, building out a suite of tools and dashboards that give them real-time visibility into key deal metrics and performance indicators.

They've also restructured their Deal Desk team to include specialized roles and responsibilities such as pricing analysts, contract managers, and data scientists. And they've implemented a rigorous training and development program to ensure that their team members have the skills and knowledge they need to succeed in a rapidly evolving environment.

As a result of these efforts, Acme Inc. has maintained a high level of speed, accuracy, and consistency in their Deal Desk operations even as they've scaled to support a multi-billion-dollar business. They've also become a model for other companies looking to adapt to Deal Desk growth and have been recognized as a leader in the industry.

2. Beta LLC

⟋ Beta LLC is a mid-size professional services firm that has recently expanded into new markets and geographies. To support this expansion, they've had to adapt their Deal Desk approach to accommodate a wider range of customer needs and expectations.

⟋ One key strategy they've employed is to create a more modular and flexible deal structure, with a range of options and add-ons that can be customized to fit the specific needs of each customer. They've also invested in building out a network of local partners and experts who can provide on-the-ground support and insights into each new market.

⟋ In addition, Beta LLC has focused on fostering a culture of collaboration and alignment across the sales, marketing, and delivery teams. They've implemented regular cross-functional meetings and workshops, where teams can share best practices and coordinate their efforts to deliver a seamless customer experience.

⟋ Through these efforts, Beta LLC has been able to adapt successfully to the challenges of growth and expansion and has seen significant improvements in customer satisfaction and retention.

3. Gamma Corp.

> Gamma Corp. is a global manufacturing company that has recently undergone a major transformation in its product and pricing strategy. To support this transformation, they've had to overhaul their Deal Desk approach and adapt to a new set of challenges and opportunities.

> One key strategy they've employed is to create a dedicated product pricing team within their Deal Desk, responsible for developing and managing pricing models and strategies across the entire product portfolio. This team works closely with product management and marketing to ensure alignment and consistency and uses advanced analytics and modeling techniques to optimize pricing for each customer segment and deal scenario.

> In addition, Gamma Corp. has invested heavily in change management and communication to align the entire organization around the new product and pricing strategy. They've implemented a comprehensive training and education program and have created a variety of forums and channels for employees to ask questions, share feedback, and stay informed about the latest developments.

> As a result of these efforts, Gamma Corp. has been able to navigate the challenges of their product and pricing transformation successfully

and has seen significant improvements in revenue growth and profitability. They've also become a model for other companies looking to adapt to major strategic shifts and have been recognized as a leader in their industry.

These examples illustrate the power of adaptation and growth in the world of Deal Desks. By investing in the right strategies, tools, and mindsets, these companies have been able to thrive in the face of major challenges and opportunities. And they serve as an inspiration for other Deal Desks looking to navigate their growth journeys.

To see how the principles of adapting to growth through effective Deal Desk management play out in the real world, let's examine the case of CyberMNO, a cybersecurity company that leveraged its Deal Desk to support rapid growth and a successful IPO.

REAL-WORLD APPLICATIONS:

Case Study: CyberMNO's Journey to IPO—Powering Growth and Compliance through Deal Desk Excellence

Background: CyberMNO, founded in the early 2000s, is a leading cybersecurity company specializing in device visibility and control. As the company experienced rapid growth in the mid-2010s, it faced increasing challenges in managing complex deals, ensuring compliance, and maintaining efficiency in its sales processes.

Challenge: As CyberMNO expanded its product offerings and customer base, the company encountered several challenges:

1. Increased deal complexity due to a diverse product portfolio

2. Growing need for consistent pricing and contracting across global markets

3. Heightened compliance requirements in preparation for going public

4. Pressure to maintain and improve deal velocity and win rates

Solution: To address these challenges, CyberMNO implemented a robust Deal Desk function. While specific details of their Deal Desk are not public, based on industry best practices, we can infer that their implementation likely included:

1. Centralized deal management: Streamlining the review and approval process for all deals above a certain threshold.

2. Standardized pricing and discounting policies: Ensuring consistency and optimizing deal values.

3. Cross-functional collaboration: Bringing together sales, finance, legal, and product teams to expedite deal closures.

4. Advanced analytics: Implementing tools to track key metrics and provide insights for continuous improvement.

5. Compliance protocols: Establishing rigorous checks to ensure all deals meet regulatory standards.

Results: The implementation of a Deal Desk coincided with significant growth and success for CyberMNO:

1. Revenue Growth: CyberMNO's revenue grew from $126.0 million in 2015 to $297.3 million in 2017, the year of their IPO—a 136% increase over two years.

2. Improved Deal Metrics: Implementing a Deal Desk improved deal cycle times, win rates, and average deal sizes.

3. Successful IPO: CyberMNO went public in October 2017, raising $116 million. The company's ability to go public demonstrates its strong financial position and compliance with regulatory requirements.

4. Scalability: The Deal Desk likely enabled CyberMNO to scale its sales operations efficiently, supporting the company's growth from a mid-size player to a public company with a billion-dollar valuation.

5. Compliance: CyberMNO must adhere to strict financial reporting and compliance standards as a public company. The Deal Desk's role in standardizing processes and ensuring thorough documentation likely played a crucial part in meeting these requirements.

Conclusion: While the specific details of CyberMNO's Deal Desk implementation are not public, the company's successful growth trajectory and IPO suggest that their deal management processes, likely centered around a robust Deal Desk, played a crucial role in their success. By streamlining complex deals, ensuring pricing consistency, and maintaining rigorous compliance standards, CyberMNO was able to scale efficiently and position itself for a successful public offering.

This case study demonstrates how a well-implemented Deal Desk can be a key driver of growth, efficiency, and compliance for high-growth technology companies preparing for major milestones such as an IPO.

CyberMNO's experience exemplifies how a well-implemented Deal Desk can drive growth, ensure compliance, and support major business milestones. By addressing the challenges of increasing deal complexity, maintaining consistency across global markets, and meeting heightened compliance requirements, CyberMNO's Deal Desk played a crucial role in the company's successful growth and IPO. This case underscores the importance of adapting your Deal Desk to support your company's evolving needs as it grows and faces new challenges.

While CyberMNO's journey illustrates the power of a well-implemented Deal Desk for a maturing company, let's examine how a Deal Desk can drive explosive growth in a younger, fast-scaling startup. The story of AI-Secure demonstrates the transformative impact of implementing a Deal Desk at a critical juncture in a company's growth trajectory.

Case Study: AI-Secure—Revolutionizing Cybersecurity and Setting IPO Records with Deal Desk Excellence

Background: AI-Secure, founded in 2013, is a pioneering cybersecurity company that uses artificial intelligence to prevent, detect, and respond to cyber threats. The company experienced explosive growth in the late 2010s and early 2020s, culminating in a record-breaking IPO in 2021.

Challenge: As AI-Secure rapidly expanded its market presence and customer base, it faced several challenges:

1. Managing a rapidly growing pipeline of complex enterprise deals

2. Ensuring consistent pricing and deal structures across diverse markets

3. Maintaining compliance and financial rigor in preparation for going public

4. Scaling sales operations to match the company's aggressive growth targets

Solution: To address these challenges and support its hypergrowth, AI-Secure implemented a Deal Desk in 2021. While specific details are not public, based on industry best practices and the company's rapid growth, we can infer that their Deal Desk implementation likely included:

1. Centralized deal management: Streamlining the review and approval process for high-value and complex deals.

2. Dynamic pricing strategies: Implementing sophisticated pricing models to optimize deal values across different market segments.

3. Cross-functional collaboration: Facilitating seamless coordination between sales, finance, legal, and product teams to accelerate deal closures.

4. Advanced analytics and AI: Leveraging cutting-edge tools to provide real-time insights and predictive analytics for deal optimization.

5. Scalable compliance frameworks: Establishing robust protocols to ensure all deals meet regulatory standards, which is crucial for a company preparing for an IPO.

Results: The implementation of the Deal Desk in 2021 coincided with AI-Secure's most impressive period of growth and its historic IPO:

1. Explosive Revenue Growth: AI-Secure's revenue grew from $93.1 million in fiscal year 2020 to $204.8 million in fiscal year 2021, a 120 percent year-over-year increase.

2. Customer Acquisition: The company's customer count increased from 4,700 to 8,100 between January 31, 2020, and April 30, 2021, demonstrating rapid market penetration supported by efficient deal management.

3. Record-breaking IPO: On June 30, 2021, AI-Secure went public in what became the highest-valued

cybersecurity IPO in history, raising $1.2 billion at a valuation of $10 billion.

4. Post-IPO Performance: In the quarter following the IPO, AI-Secure reported a 121 percent year-over-year revenue growth, suggesting that the Deal Desk continued to drive efficiency and growth post-public offering.

5. Scalability and Efficiency: The Deal Desk played a crucial role in enabling AI-Secure to scale its sales operations rapidly, supporting the company's transition from a fast-growing startup to a public company leader in the cybersecurity space.

6. Compliance and Investor Confidence: The successful IPO and subsequent performance indicate strong financial management and compliance practices, areas where a well-implemented Deal Desk typically excels.

Conclusion: While the specific impact of AI-Secure's Deal Desk is not publicly available, the timing of its implementation in 2021 aligns perfectly with the company's most impressive period of growth and its historic IPO. By streamlining complex enterprise deals, ensuring pricing optimization, and maintaining rigorous compliance standards, the Deal Desk played a crucial role in AI-Secure's ability to scale efficiently and position itself for the most successful cybersecurity IPO in history.

This case study underscores how a strategically implemented Deal Desk can be a key driver of hypergrowth, operational efficiency, and market success for high-growth technology companies, particularly in the lead-up to significant events like an IPO. AI-Secure's record-breaking performance serves as a powerful testament to the potential impact of excellent deal management practices.

AI-Secure's experience further reinforces the critical role of a Deal Desk in managing rapid growth and preparing for major milestones like an IPO. It exemplifies how the strategies we've discussed—from centralizing deal management to leveraging advanced analytics—can be applied to achieve extraordinary results quickly. This case also underscores the importance of timing in Deal Desk implementation, showing how even a relatively new Deal Desk can have a significant impact when aligned with a company's growth phase and strategic objectives.

CONCLUSION

As we've seen throughout this chapter, adapting to Deal Desk growth is no easy feat, as it demands commitment and stamina. It requires a combination of strategic vision, operational excellence, and sheer determination—not to mention a willingness to embrace change and uncertainty.

Every Deal Desk will face its fair share of challenges, from complex negotiations to unexpected roadblocks. The key is to approach these challenges with resilience and a problem-solving mindset.

*It ain't about how hard you hit. It's about how
hard you can get hit and keep moving forward.*

—Rocky Balboa

When challenges arise, remember that they are opportunities
in disguise. Each obstacle you overcome makes your Deal
Desk stronger and more capable. By maintaining a positive
attitude and a relentless drive to find solutions, you can turn
challenges into stepping stones to success.

For those Deal Desks that can rise to the challenge, the
rewards are significant. By successfully navigating the twists
and turns of growth and expansion, you can unlock new levels
of success and impact for your business and position yourself
as a leader in your industry.

So, as you embark on your own Deal Desk growth journey,
remember the key strategies and best practices we've explored
in this chapter. Streamline and automate your processes, invest
in data and analytics, foster a culture of continuous learning
and improvement, collaborate and align with other teams, and
always stay customer-centric.

Above all, remember that growth and adaptation are not a
destination but a journey. There will always be new challenges
and opportunities to navigate and new plot twists and turns to
overcome. But with the right mindset and approach, you can
turn those challenges into opportunities and those plot twists
into the stuff of Deal Desk legend.

So, here's to your Deal Desk growth journey—may it be filled with success, learning, and plenty of popcorn-worthy moments along the way. May you always remember that no matter how big the screen or how bright the lights are, the true stars of the show are the people and teams behind the scenes working tirelessly to make the magic happen.

Cut. That's a wrap…for now.

CHAPTER 11

CONTINUOUS IMPROVEMENT

Continuous improvement is at the heart of successful Deal Desk management. It requires resilience, adaptability, and a willingness to learn from both successes and failures. A personal experience from my college days perfectly illustrates these principles. I'm about to take you on a linguistic rollercoaster that'll make your high school French class look like a walk in the park.

The two summers spent in France, diving from heart-stopping heights into pools that were about as deep as a kiddie pool (talk about living on the edge!), were amazing. My experience with the international high-diving team was as thrilling as it was terrifying. My high school French was put to the test, and I came out speaking like a local ... or so I thought.

Fast forward to my return to the States. I was pumped, I was confident, and I was ready to take my French to the next level. So, what did I do? I signed up for the linguistic equivalent of running a marathon while juggling flaming torches—an advanced French class that crammed three terms into one. Ooh la la, indeed!

Now, here's where it gets interesting. I strutted into class, all smiles and 'bonjours,' ready to dazzle my new professor with my newly acquired French flair. But faster than you can say 'croissant,' I realized I'd stepped into a real-life version of *Mean Girls*—except it was just one mean girl, and she was the professor.

From day one, this professor had it out for me. Maybe it was because I mentioned my time in France, or perhaps she just didn't like me or how I spoke. Whatever the reason, I was suddenly persona non grata in a class of fourteen. Fourteen! And yet, no matter how many times I raised my hand, she looked past me like I was invisible. Talk about a French disconnection!

I tried everything—extra lab work, workbooks, you name it. But nothing worked. It was like trying to win a popularity contest with Marie Antoinette. When I tried to drop the class, the dean basically told me to eat cake (or in this case, a box of tissues).

But here's the thing about setbacks—they're just setups for comebacks. I may have stopped attending that class, but I didn't give up on French. Nope, I doubled down. Next term, I retook the class with a new professor, crossing my fingers that history wouldn't repeat itself.

And then, like a scene from a feel-good movie, my new professor walked in carrying a Contempo Casuals shopping bag. Now, if you recall, you'll remember that's where I'd been working full-time through college. It was like the universe was finally throwing me a bone—in the form of a Montreal native who appreciated both French and fashion.

Long story short, I aced that class and achieved a 3.5 grade. But more importantly, I learned a valuable lesson: Sometimes, you've got to weather the storm to appreciate the rainbow. Or, in this case, survive the reign of terror to enjoy the reign of chic. Oh, and let's not forget—not paying attention to deadlines can be a costly mistake. Missing that drop deadline was like trying to return a designer dress after the big event—it just doesn't work, folks!

So, the next time you face a seemingly insurmountable challenge, remember my French fiasco. Keep pushing, keep trying, and who knows? Your next big break might just walk through the door carrying a shopping bag from your favorite store. Perseverance, mes amis, is the secret ingredient in the recipe for success—whether you're diving from great heights, learning a new language, or navigating the complex world of Deal Desks!

This experience encapsulates key aspects of continuous improvement that are crucial in Deal Desk operations:

1. Resilience in the face of setbacks: Just as I didn't let my initial negative experience deter me from mastering

French, Deal Desk professionals must persist through challenges and setbacks.

2. **Willingness to try again:** Retaking the class demonstrates the importance of not giving up after initial failures—a crucial mindset in the ever-evolving world of deal management.

3. **Learning from experience:** The contrast between my two experiences shows how we can apply lessons from past challenges to improve future outcomes.

Let's explore how these principles of continuous improvement can be applied to elevate your Deal Desk operations.

Fade in on a world-class movie studio, where the best and brightest minds in the business are hard at work crafting the next big blockbuster. The sets are buzzing with activity, the cameras are rolling, and the energy is palpable. But amidst all the hustle and bustle, there's one thing that sets this studio apart from the rest: a relentless commitment to continuous improvement.

You see, in the world of filmmaking—just like in the world of Deal Desks—success is not a one-time achievement but an ongoing process of learning, iterating, and pushing the boundaries of what's possible. The most successful studios are the ones that are never content to rest on their laurels but are always looking for ways to improve their craft, streamline their processes, and deliver even greater value to their audiences.

It is the same with your Deal Desk. As you've navigated the challenges of growth and scaled your operations to new heights, you've undoubtedly achieved some incredible successes along the way. But the journey of continuous improvement is never really finished. There's always more to learn, optimize, and achieve.

So let's explore continuous improvement in the context of Deal Desks. We'll delve into the key principles and practices that underpin a culture of ongoing optimization and provide a roadmap for embedding continuous improvement into the very fabric of your Deal Desk operations. Along the way, we'll cover illustrative examples and case studies of Deal Desks that have successfully embraced the never-ending quest for excellence and reaped the rewards that come with it.

Grab your director's chair and get ready for the next scene in your Deal Desk journey. It's time to cut through the clutter, zoom in on what really matters, and write the script for a future of unstoppable continuous improvement.

THE PRINCIPLES OF CONTINUOUS IMPROVEMENT

At its core, continuous improvement is about one thing: the relentless pursuit of excellence. It's about never being satisfied with the status quo, and always striving to be better tomorrow than you were today. But what does that look like in practice? What are the key principles that underpin a culture of continuous improvement in the world of Deal Desks?

1. Customer-centricity

    > The first and most important principle of continuous improvement is customer-centricity. Your Deal Desk exists to serve your customers— to help them achieve their goals, solve their problems, and drive their success.

    > To truly embrace continuous improvement, you need to put your customers at the center of everything you do. That means constantly seeking their feedback and insights, using that feedback to guide your optimization efforts, and always asking yourself: "How can we deliver even more value to our customers?"

2. Data-driven decision-making

    > Another key principle of continuous improvement is data-driven decision-making. In a world of constant change and uncertainty, gut instincts and hunches will only get you so far. To truly optimize your Deal Desk operations, you need to rely on hard data and objective metrics.

    > That means investing in robust data collection and analysis capabilities, using that data to identify trends and patterns, and making decisions based on evidence rather than assumptions. It also means being willing to experiment and test new

ideas and using the results to inform your ongoing optimization efforts.

3. Cross-functional collaboration

> Continuous improvement is not a solo endeavor—it requires collaboration and alignment across your entire organization. Your Deal Desk does not operate in a vacuum; it is deeply interconnected with a wide range of other teams and functional areas, from sales and marketing to product and finance.

> To drive true continuous improvement, you need to break down silos and foster a culture of cross-functional collaboration. That means building strong relationships and communication channels with other teams, seeking their input and expertise, and working together to identify and solve problems.

4. Iterative and incremental approach

> Continuous improvement is not about big, dramatic changes—it's about small, incremental improvements that add up over time. It's about breaking down complex problems into manageable pieces and tackling them one step at a time.

 To embrace this principle, you need to adopt an iterative and incremental approach to optimization. That means focusing on small, achievable goals, testing and refining your ideas along the way, and celebrating the progress you make, no matter how small. Over time, those minor improvements will compound into big results.

5. Continuous learning and growth

 Finally, continuous improvement is about continuous learning and growth. It's about recognizing that there's always more to learn, discover, and achieve. It's about fostering a culture of curiosity, experimentation, and risk-taking.

 To truly embrace this principle, you need to invest in the ongoing development and growth of your team. That means providing them with the training, coaching, and resources they need to expand their skills and knowledge and creating opportunities for them to take on new challenges and stretch beyond their comfort zones.

By embracing these principles and embedding them into the DNA of your Deal Desk culture, you can create a powerful engine for ongoing optimization and growth. But principles alone are not enough—you also need a clear roadmap for putting them into practice.

THE CONTINUOUS IMPROVEMENT ROADMAP

So, what does the path to continuous improvement look like in practice? How can you take the principles we've discussed and turn them into a concrete plan of action? Here's a roadmap to guide your journey:

1. Assess your current state

   - The first step in any continuous improvement journey is to assess your current state. That means taking an honest, objective look at your Deal Desk operations, and identifying your strengths, weaknesses, and opportunities for improvement.

   - This assessment should be data-driven and comprehensive, covering everything from your processes and systems to your people and culture. Use a variety of tools and techniques—such as surveys, interviews, and process mapping—to gather input from a wide range of stakeholders and use that input to create a clear picture of where you are today so you will know where you need to go.

2. Set your goals and priorities

> Once you have a clear understanding of your current state, the next step is to set your goals and priorities for improvement. What are the most important areas for optimization? Which metrics will you use to track your progress? What outcomes do you want to achieve?

> Be specific, measurable, and realistic in your goal-setting. Focus on the areas that will have the biggest impact on your customers and your business, and align your goals with your overall Deal Desk strategy and vision.

3. Develop your action plan

> With your goals and priorities in place, it's time to develop your action plan. This is where you'll translate your high-level objectives into specific, actionable steps and initiatives.

> Break down your goals into smaller, more manageable pieces, and assign clear owners and timelines for each piece. Identify the resources and support you'll need to execute your plan and put in place the necessary structures and processes to ensure accountability and follow-through.

4. Execute and iterate

  - Now it's time to put your plan into action. This is where the rubber meets the road, and where the actual work of continuous improvement begins.

  - As you execute your initiatives, be prepared to adapt and iterate along the way. Use data and feedback to track your progress, identify what's working and what's not, and adjust as needed. Celebrate your successes, learn from your failures, and keep pushing forward.

5. Measure and optimize

  - Finally, the key to sustaining your continuous improvement efforts over time is to measure and optimize your results. Use the metrics and KPIs you identified in your goal-setting phase to track your progress and use that data to drive ongoing optimization and refinement.

  - Look for patterns and trends in your data and use those insights to identify new opportunities for improvement. Share your results and learnings with your team and stakeholders and use them to build momentum and buy-in for your ongoing efforts.

By following this roadmap and embedding continuous improvement into the fabric of your Deal Desk culture, you can create a powerful engine for ongoing optimization and growth. But the path to excellence is not always a smooth one—there will be challenges and obstacles along the way.

OVERCOMING THE CHALLENGES OF CONTINUOUS IMPROVEMENT

As with any major organizational change effort, embracing continuous improvement in your Deal Desk is not without its challenges. Here are some of the most common obstacles you may face, and some strategies for overcoming them:

1. Resistance to change

    ⌐ One of the biggest challenges of continuous improvement is resistance to change. People are naturally resistant to change and may be skeptical of new ideas or initiatives that disrupt the status quo.

    ⌐ To overcome this resistance, it's important to communicate the "why" behind your continuous improvement efforts. Help your team understand the benefits of ongoing optimization—for your customers, for your business, and for them personally. Involve them in the process, seek their input and feedback, and celebrate their successes along the way.

2. Lack of resources or prioritization

    ⌐ Another common challenge is a lack of resources or prioritization. With so many competing demands on your time and attention, it's difficult to carve out the capacity and budget needed for continuous improvement.

, To overcome this challenge, it's important to make continuous improvement a strategic priority for your Deal Desk, and to allocate the resources and support to make it happen. Look for ways to optimize your existing resources and make the case for additional investment where needed.

3. Siloed thinking and lack of collaboration

, Continuous improvement often requires breaking down silos and fostering cross-functional collaboration—but this can be easier said than done. Different teams and functional areas may have different goals, incentives, and ways of working, making it difficult to align and coordinate efforts.

, To overcome this challenge, it's important to build strong relationships and communication channels across your organization. Foster a culture of trust, transparency, and shared purpose, and create opportunities for teams to work together and learn from each other.

4. Short-term thinking and lack of patience

> Continuous improvement is a long-term game—it requires patience, persistence, and a willingness to play the long game. But in a world of short-term pressures and quick wins, it can be tempting to prioritize immediate results over lasting change.

> To overcome this challenge, it's important to balance short-term and long-term thinking in your continuous improvement efforts. Celebrate the quick wins and incremental improvements along the way, but never lose sight of the bigger picture and the long-term vision you're working toward.

By anticipating and proactively addressing these challenges, you can create a more resilient and sustainable continuous improvement culture in your Deal Desk. But the journey doesn't end there—in fact, it's just the beginning.

To ensure your Deal Desk team stays at the cutting edge of best practices, consider ongoing professional development. Deal Solutions will offer comprehensive training programs and support for Deal Desk and deal management professionals, helping teams continuously enhance their skills and knowledge.

CONTINUOUS IMPROVEMENT IN ACTION: A DEAL DESK EXAMPLE

To bring the power of continuous improvement to life, let's examine an example of a Deal Desk that has successfully embraced the never-ending quest for excellence.

We are revisiting Acme Inc., the fast-growing enterprise software company that has built a reputation for innovation and customer-centricity, but as the company scaled and its Deal Desk operations became more complex, the team struggled with inefficiencies, inconsistencies, and a lack of alignment across different functional areas.

To address these challenges, Acme's Deal Desk leadership team embarked on a continuous improvement journey. They started by conducting a comprehensive assessment of their current state, gathering input from a wide range of stakeholders, and using data to identify key areas for optimization.

Based on this assessment, they set clear goals and priorities for improvement, focusing on three key areas: streamlining their processes, enhancing their data and analytics capabilities, and fostering a culture of cross-functional collaboration.

To streamline their processes, they launched a major initiative to standardize and automate key workflows, such as pricing approvals and contract generation. They invested in new tools and technologies to support these efforts and worked closely with their respective teams to ensure seamless integration and adoption.

To enhance their data and analytics capabilities, they built a robust data infrastructure and reporting platform, which gave them real-time visibility into key metrics and performance indicators. They also hired a dedicated data analyst to help them make sense of all this data and identify trends and opportunities for optimization.

To foster a culture of cross-functional collaboration, they launched a series of workshops and initiatives, bringing together teams from across the organization to solve problems and drive innovation. They also implemented new communication and collaboration tools, such as Slack and Asana, to help teams work together more effectively.

As they executed these initiatives, Acme's Deal Desk team was relentless in their focus on continuous improvement. They tracked their progress obsessively, using data and feedback to identify what was working and what wasn't, and iterating rapidly based on what they learned.

Over time, these efforts paid off in a big way. Acme's Deal Desk saw significant improvements in key metrics like cycle times, win rate, and customer satisfaction. They also saw a marked increase in cross-functional alignment and collaboration, with teams working together more seamlessly than ever before.

But perhaps most importantly, Acme's Deal Desk team developed a true culture of continuous improvement—a shared mindset and way of working that prioritized ongoing optimization and growth above all else. They became known throughout the organization as a team that was always pushing the boundaries of what was possible, and inspiring others to do the same.

Today, Acme's Deal Desk is held up as a model of excellence within the company and beyond. But the team knows that their work is never done. They continue to push forward on their continuous improvement journey, always looking for new ways to learn, grow, and deliver even more value to their customers and their business.

CONCLUSION

And so, we come to the end of our journey through the world of Deal Desks—a journey that has taken us from the bright lights of Hollywood to the trenches of enterprise software and everywhere in between.

Along the way, we've explored the many facets of Deal Desk excellence—from the art of assembling a rock star team, to the science of optimizing processes and systems, to the never-ending quest for continuous improvement. We've seen how the most successful Deal Desks are the ones that never stop learning, growing, and pushing the boundaries of what's possible.

But perhaps the most important lesson of all is this: in the world of Deal Desks, as in the world of movies, the story is never really over. There's always another scene to shoot, challenge to overcome, or opportunity to seize. The key is to embrace that never-ending journey and to find joy and purpose in the pursuit of excellence.

As you leave this book and return to your own Deal Desk journey, remember the principles and practices we've explored along the way. Put your customers at the center of everything you do, use data to guide your decisions, collaborate across functional areas, iterate and experiment relentlessly, and never stop learning and growing.

And above all, remember that the true measure of your success is not in the deals you close or the metrics you hit, but in the value you create for your customers, your business, and the world around you. That's the real magic of Deal Desks—the ability to transform the way business gets done and to make a real difference in the lives of the people you serve.

So, here's to your never-ending quest for Deal Desk excellence—may it be filled with twists and turns, triumphs and tribulations, and plenty of popcorn-worthy moments along the way. And may you always remember that, in the end, the most important story you'll ever tell is the one you write yourself.

Fade to black. Roll credits.

PART 5

AFTER CREDITS— THE HUMAN ELEMENT: BUILDING A WORLD-CLASS DEAL DESK CULTURE

CHAPTER 12

BUILDING A CULTURE OF INNOVATION

Welcome to the grand finale of our Deal Desk adventure! Let's dive (pun intended) into a topic that's the secret sauce to our success: creating a culture of innovation and collaborative problem-solving.

> *We all get to the peak together, or*
> *we don't get there at all.*
>
> —*Hidden Figures*

Imagine this: You're at a potluck dinner. There are twenty dishes, but they're all macaroni and cheese. Sure, mac and cheese is awesome, but twenty variations of the same thing? Boring! Now, picture that same potluck with a variety of dishes. Spicy tacos, savory sushi, hearty lasagna—you get the idea. That's the power of different perspectives and experiences. It brings a richness of ideas that makes everything better.

At Adobe, we had a "Most Innovative Idea" contest that was like the Olympics for ideas. Picture a room buzzing with excitement, with everyone from interns to executives submitting their brainwaves. One idea of mine once took home the gold, and another nabbed the silver. But here's the kicker—it wasn't just about winning. The real magic was seeing how this contest brought out the best in everyone, regardless of their job title.

The contest was open to all, and it was amazing to see how many brilliant ideas came from unexpected places. It was like finding a gourmet chef at a hotdog stand. People with different experiences and perspectives contributed to game-changing innovations that cost next to nothing but had a tremendous impact. It was inspiring and empowering to see everyone make a significant difference, no matter their role.

So, how does this relate to our Deal Desk? Simple. By fostering a culture of innovation and collaboration, we're creating a powerhouse of creativity and problem-solving prowess. It's about bringing together different perspectives and letting the magic happen.

Let's be clear: varied perspectives aren't just nice to have— they're a strategic advantage. Research shows that teams with different viewpoints and experiences are more innovative and better at solving complex problems. They spot opportunities and pitfalls that a team with similar backgrounds might miss. It's like having a multi-lingual GPS in a city where every street sign is in a different language. You'll never get lost!

In our Deal Desk, this means encouraging open dialogue, valuing every voice, and celebrating the unique contributions of each team member. It's about creating a safe space where everyone feels empowered to share their ideas and where collaboration sparks innovation.

The real magic of a strong team culture lies in the way it transforms our dynamics and outcomes. When people feel valued and heard, they're more likely to contribute their best ideas and efforts. This creates a positive feedback loop, where the success of one initiative inspires even more extraordinary contributions and innovations.

Creating this kind of environment requires commitment and intentionality. It's about more than just policies and procedures; it's about building a culture where everyone feels they can contribute. This means actively seeking out different perspectives, encouraging open dialogue, and ensuring that every team member has the opportunity to shine.

In conclusion, fostering innovation and collaboration are not just key components of our Deal Desk's success; they are the foundation upon which we build our future. By embracing these principles, we unlock the full potential of our team and set ourselves up for sustained success.

CHAPTER 13

SOFT SKILLS

Welcome to the jazz club of deal-making, where soft skills sync up the rhythm, and everyone's got a part to play! We're not just talking tactics; we're diving into the emotional jam session that makes a Deal Desk truly groove. So, grab your metaphorical saxophone, and let's make some sweet, sweet music together. We'll explore how to complement the diverse team with the soft skills necessary to navigate the complex human dynamics of deal-making. Get ready to master the art of Deal Desk diplomacy!

> *Music can change the world because*
> *it can change people.*
>
> —*Bono, U2*

Just like a captivating melody can transform an audience, the right mix of soft skills can revolutionize your Deal Desk. Let me tell you a story: One sunny Tuesday, I found myself in a sticky situation with Kendra, one of my direct reports. Kendra was a hard worker and always kind, but things had been slipping through the cracks. Her role wasn't playing to her strengths, and as her manager, I had a choice. I could focus on the negatives, or I could pivot and turn this into a positive.

I chose the latter. Instead of zooming in on the slips, I highlighted Kendra's strengths during our chat. We explored what she loved doing and where she truly shined. It was more than just a check-in; it was a chance to realign her career path toward something that sparked her passion. I even had a list of open positions that would suit her better. Kendra was not just relieved; she was reinvigorated. She transitioned to a role where she could thrive, and our team's rhythm got a whole lot smoother.

NEEDED SKILLS

Now, let's jazz up your understanding of the critical soft skills that can make or break your Deal Desk's effectiveness.

Effective Communication Across Departments and Hierarchies

Imagine the Deal Desk as a band conductor, weaving through the various sounds of the sales, legal, and finance teams. Here's how you keep the music flowing:

- **Tailor Your Message:** Speak everyone's language. Serenade finance with return on investment (ROI) tunes and woo sales with catchy value propositions.

It's like being a linguistic chameleon, adapting your communication style to resonate with each department's unique frequency.

- **Active Listening:** Be all ears. Jazz and business are as much about listening as they are playing. Think of it as tuning your instrument to match the orchestra around you—you'll create beautiful harmony when you're perfectly in sync with your colleagues.

- **Clear and Concise Messaging:** Keep your solos short and sweet. In a fast-paced environment, no one has time for a drum solo. Think of your messages as catchy pop songs—they should be memorable, impactful, and leave your audience wanting more.

- **Storytelling:** Turn your data into a riveting narrative. Make your audience feel the beat, not just hear the notes. It's like turning a dry financial report into a blockbuster movie—with the right storytelling, even the most complex deal can become a page-turner.

Emotional Intelligence in High-Stakes Negotiations

Negotiations are like intricate dance routines. Here's how you stay graceful under pressure:

- **Self-Awareness & Self-Regulation:** Know your (dance) moves and keep your cool when the tempo changes. Be like a tango dancer who can adjust their steps fluidly, even when the music suddenly switches to salsa.

- **Empathy:** Tune into the emotional wavelengths of others. Have an emotional radar that helps you navigate the choppy waters of high-stakes negotiations. The more accurately you can read the room, the better you can steer the ship.

- **Social Skills:** Smooth talking goes a long way in building rapport and navigating complex dynamics. Think of it as being the life of the party—but instead of just making small talk, you're creating connections that can make or break million-dollar deals.

Conflict Resolution and Stakeholder Management

When the band disagrees on which tune, it's your job to harmonize:

- **Focus on Interests, Not Positions:** It's like finding the harmony in discord. Instead of getting stuck on who plays what instrument, focus on creating beautiful music together. You might find that seemingly opposing interests can create unexpected and delightful compositions.

- **Use "Yes, and..." Instead of "But":** Keep adding to the music, don't stop the flow. It's like a jazz improvisation session—build on what others contribute rather than shutting down their ideas.

This approach can turn potential conflicts into collaborative masterpieces.

- **Seek Win-Win Solutions:** Ensure everyone leaves the jam session feeling like they've had a solo and time to shine. It's about creating an arrangement where every instrument gets its moment in the spotlight, resulting in a performance that's greater than the sum of its parts.

- **Know When to Escalate:** Sometimes, you need to bring in the big guns (or, in our case, the big drums). It's like knowing when to bring in the conductor to resolve a dispute in the orchestra. Timing is everything—escalate too soon, and you undermine your authority; too late, and the performance suffers.

Building Trust and Credibility

Trust is like fan loyalty; it takes time to build but is essential for a lasting career:

- **Consistency:** Be the metronome that always keeps time. In the world of deals, being reliable is your superpower. It's like being the bassist in a band—you might not always be in the spotlight, but you're the foundation that everyone else relies on.

- **Transparency:** Let your bandmates know the setlist ahead of time. In deal-making, surprises are rarely welcome. Think of transparency as sharing your game plan with the team—when everyone knows what's coming, they can prepare and perform at their best.

- **Competence:** Keep sharpening your skills, whether it's scales or scat singing. In the ever-evolving world of deal-making, continuous learning is your ticket to stardom. It's like a musician who practices daily—the more you hone your craft, the more impressive your performance becomes.

- **Vulnerability:** Show you're human. Even virtuosos hit a wrong note now and then. Admitting mistakes and showing vulnerability isn't a weakness—it's a strength that builds authentic connections. It's like a rock star sharing their personal struggles—it makes them more relatable and often endears them more to their fans.

Adaptability and Resilience

The deal world is constantly changing. Here's how you stay on your toes:

- **Embrace a Growth Mindset:** Each challenge is just a new riff waiting to be mastered. Approach each deal as a learning opportunity, and you'll find yourself improving with every performance. It again matches the musician who sees each gig as a chance to experiment and grow.

- **Stay Curious:** Keep exploring new genres and styles. In deal-making, this means staying abreast of new industries, technologies, and deal structures. It's like a DJ who's always on the hunt for the next big sound—your curiosity keeps your deals fresh and innovative.

- **Practice Flexibility:** Sometimes, you switch from jazz to blues mid-set. Go with it. The ability to pivot quickly is crucial in deal-making. Think of it as being a musical shapeshifter—the more styles you can play, the more valuable you become to the band.

- **Develop Coping Strategies:** Find your backstage zen amid the festival chaos. Deal-making can be stressful, so it's crucial to have techniques to maintain your cool. It's like having pre-show rituals that center you before a big performance—find what works for you and make it a habit.

DEVELOPING YOUR SOFT SKILLS

Think of this as your ongoing gig. Set goals, seek feedback, and jam with mentors. Keep learning, whether through books, workshops, or live sessions. The more versatile you are, the more indispensable you become to any band—or Deal Desk.

CONCLUSION: THE DIPLOMATIC DEAL DESK PROFESSIONAL

You're not just a deal maker; you're a maestro of human dynamics. By tuning up your soft skills, you enhance not just your career but the entire ensemble's performance. So, take center stage, cue the spotlight, and let's make some deal music happen!

CHAPTER 14

TRANSFORMATIONAL LEADERSHIP

Welcome to the grand finale of our Deal Desk journey—where leadership isn't just about managing, it's about transforming! Picture yourself not just as a leader, but as a magician, where every flourish of your wand (okay, your spreadsheet) brings out the best in your team.

Innovation distinguishes between
a leader and a follower.

—*Steve Jobs*

As we explore the realm of transformational leadership, remember that it's the innovators, visionaries, and daring leaders who not only pave new paths but also lead their teams along them. Let's dive into how you can be that transformational leader, turning everyday operations into strategic victories and molding your Deal Desk into a powerhouse of progress.

THE TALE OF THE TRANSFORMATIONAL TURNAROUND

Once upon a time at TheGianTech, there was a Deal Desk that felt more like a bottleneck than a boost. Enter Gretchen, a leader with a cape (metaphorically speaking) and a vision. But before we dive into how Gretchen transformed her team from lagging to legendary, let's explore the magic tricks (a.k.a. transformational leadership skills) she used.

Visionary Vibes

Imagine envisioning a world where your Deal Desk isn't just a cog in the machine but the engine driving the company forward. That's what visionary leaders do. They see beyond the daily grind to what could be. Like a director of a blockbuster, they set the scene for epic achievements.

Story time with Gretchen: When she took the helm, Gretchen painted a vivid picture of a Deal Desk that worked like a well-oiled machine—speedy, efficient, and innovative. Her team didn't just buy into this vision; they became co-creators of it.

Inspirational Motivation

It's one thing to have a vision; it's another to get everyone jazzed about it. Transformational leaders are the ultimate hype people—they can rally their team with just the right words and energy.

Gretchen's Pep Talks: Like a coach before the big game, Gretchen's motivational speeches didn't just inspire her team; they sparked a fire. Her secret? She always linked the day-to-day work with the big-picture impact, making every task feel epic.

Culture of Learning and Innovation

In Gretchen's team, learning was as routine as morning coffee. She fostered an environment where trying new things and sometimes failing was not just accepted, but celebrated.

Fail Forward Fridays: Once a month, Gretchen hosted a session where the team would dissect mistakes, not to assign blame, but to learn and grow. These sessions became so popular that they were live-streamed across departments!

Continuous Growth

A true transformational leader doesn't just develop their business; they develop their people. Gretchen made sure her team had access to training, workshops, and especially cross-functional projects that stretched their skills and broadened their horizons.

Mentorship Magic: Gretchen paired up team members from different departments, turning the Deal Desk into a mentorship hub. This not only upskilled her team but also broke down silos within the company.

The Art of Alignment

Gretchen understood that for her Deal Desk to truly succeed, it needed to align seamlessly with the broader organizational goals. She didn't keep her strategies a secret; she shared them with every C-suite exec, ensuring the Deal Desk's objectives were everyone's objectives.

Strategic Coffee Chats: Gretchen made it her mission to have coffee with a different exec each week, discussing not just current deals but strategic goals. These informal chats ensured the Deal Desk was always in tune with the company's heartbeat.

Cultivating Tomorrow's Trailblazers

Every visionary leader shines not by their lone accomplishments, but by the legacy of leaders they cultivate along their journey. Gretchen was not just at the helm of the Deal Desk; she was the chief architect behind a vibrant leadership nursery.

Leadership Incubator Initiative: Gretchen pioneered the "Leadership Incubator," an innovative program designed for emerging leaders within her team. This initiative was more than a series of training sessions; it was a dynamic ecosystem where potential leaders could germinate their skills.

Under Gretchen's guidance, the Leadership Incubator offered a blend of hands-on projects and mentorship opportunities. Participants engaged in real-world challenges, applying their skills to streamline processes, negotiate complex deals, and drive strategic initiatives. They weren't just learning about leadership; they were practicing it in real-time, under the careful guidance of seasoned executives.

Shadowing sessions were a cornerstone of this program, where aspirants could step into the shoes of senior leaders, attending high-level meetings and contributing to critical decision-making processes. This immersion provided them with invaluable insights into the nuances of strategic leadership and the complexities of managing a top-tier Deal Desk.

This proactive approach did more than prepare the next generation of leaders—it ensured the sustainability and ongoing evolution of the Deal Desk. Gretchen's foresight in developing this program meant that the organization was continually rejuvenating its leadership pipeline, fostering a culture of continuous improvement and ambitious growth.

The Transformational Turnaround: By the time Gretchen was done, the Deal Desk had cut deal cycle times in half, doubled its deal size, and, most importantly, had an empowered, motivated, and driven team. TheGianTech now cites the Deal Desk as a key differentiator in its market success.

CURTAIN CLOSE CONCLUSION: THE TRANSFORMATIONAL IMPERATIVE

As we conclude our journey through the world of Deal Desks, remember this: in today's rapidly changing business landscape, transformation is not just an option—it's imperative. By embracing transformational leadership, you have the power to elevate your Deal Desk from a support function to a strategic driver of organizational success.

Your Deal Desk can be more than just a processor of transactions. It can be a hub of innovation, driver of strategic insights, and catalyst for organizational growth. The journey may be challenging, but the rewards—for you, your team, and your organization—are immense.

So, as you close this book and think about your current deal management processes, ask yourself: What's your vision for transformation? What's the first step you'll take on this adventure? The future of deal-making is in your hands. Make it extraordinary.

Whether you're just starting your Deal Desk journey or looking to optimize an existing function, remember that expert support is available. Deal Solutions offers various services, from virtual Deal Desk support to complete Deal Desk buildouts, training, and ongoing optimization. Whatever your Deal Desk needs, there are resources available to help you succeed.

GLOSSARY OF KEY TERMS

1. Application Programming Interface (API): A set of defined rules and protocols that enable different software systems to communicate with each other.

2. Approval Workflow: The process by which relevant parties review and approve deals within an organization.

3. Continuous Improvement: An ongoing effort to improve products, services, or processes.

4. Contract Lifecycle Management (CLM): The process of managing a contract from initiation through award, compliance, and renewal.

5. CPQ (Configure, Price, Quote): Software that helps sales teams produce accurate and highly configured quotes.

6. CRM (Customer Relationship Management): A system for managing a company's interactions with current and potential customers.

7. Cross-functional Collaboration: The process of different departments or teams working together toward a common goal.

8. Customer Satisfaction: A measure of how products and services supplied by a company meet or surpass customer expectations.

9. Data Governance: A comprehensive framework of policies, procedures, and standards that organizations implement to ensure the effective management, quality, security, and usability of their data assets throughout their lifecycle.

10. Deal Analytics: The use of data analysis to gain insights into deal performance and make data-driven decisions.

11. Deal Cycle Time: The average time it takes to complete a deal from start to finish.

12. Deal Desk: A centralized function within an organization that manages and optimizes complex sales deals, typically involving cross-functional collaboration.

13. Deal Velocity: The speed at which a deal moves through the sales pipeline from initial contact to closure.

14. ERP (Enterprise Resource Planning systems): A type of software that integrates all business functions and processes into one system. It helps

organizations manage and coordinate their operations, including financials, human resources, supply chain management, and more.

15. KPI (Key Performance Indicator): A measurable value that demonstrates how effectively a company is achieving key business objectives.

16. Pricing Accuracy: The degree to which actual prices align with intended pricing strategies and policies.

17. Pricing Strategy: The method a company uses to price its products or services.

18. RACI Matrix: A responsibility assignment chart that clarifies roles and responsibilities in cross-functional processes. Each role involved in a process is assigned as responsible, accountable, consulted, or informed based on their level of involvement and responsibility.

19. ROI: Return on Investment: A financial metric used to evaluate the effectiveness of an investment or a particular initiative.

20. Revenue Recognition: The process of recognizing revenue in financial statements according to specific accounting rules.

21. SLA (Service Level Agreement): A commitment between a service provider and a client, often detailing the level of service expected.

22. SMART Goals: Specific, measurable, achievable, realistic, time-bound goals that are designed to be actionable.

23. Stakeholder Management: The process of managing the expectations and engagement of individuals or groups who have an interest in a project or business.

24. Transformational Leadership: A leadership approach that causes change in individuals and social systems, creating valuable and positive change in followers.

25. Win Rate: The percentage of deals that result in a sale compared to the total number of deals pursued.

ACKNOWLEDGMENTS

To my **friends and family**, whose unwavering encouragement and love have been my foundation. Your support has lifted me in moments of doubt and fueled my journey forward.

To **Allison Davis**, my coach, whose guidance led me to recognize the power of sharing my Deal Desk expertise. Your insight and encouragement helped transform my experience into a resource for others.

To **Robin Hall**, whose dedication to reading aloud with me has refined and elevated this book beyond measure. Your patience and attention to detail have made an immeasurable difference.

To **David Thompson**, whose belief in this work brought forth a foreword perfectly capturing its essence and purpose. Your contribution is invaluable.

Thank you to **Katie Chambers and Em Syth** of **Beacon Point LLC** for your editorial expertise and keen attention to detail. Your insights and guidance helped refine this book, and I appreciate your dedication to making it the best it can be.

Thank you to **Carly Catt** of **Catt Editing, LLC,** for your proofreading, valuable feedback, and keen eye for detail. Your thoughtful suggestions and corrections significantly improved the quality of this manuscript.

Thank you all for being part of this journey—this book would not be the same without you.

AUTHOR BIO

Meet Jill Roman, the Deal Desk dynamo who's been turning chaos into revenue-generating magic for over a decade. With a career spanning legal, finance, revenue operations, auditing, and accounting, Jill has become the go-to guru for companies looking to supercharge their deal processes and skyrocket their growth.

Jill's expertise is backed by impressive academic credentials and a stellar career trajectory. She holds a Master of Business Administration, graduating Summa Cum Laude from Siena Heights University, and is a certified Master Business Consulting Professional from the International Association of Professions Career College.

Her professional journey includes pivotal roles at some of the tech industry's most influential companies, including Adobe Systems, Netflix, Oracle, SentinelOne, Macrovision, and Forescout. This breadth of experience across diverse business models and scales gives Jill a unique, 360-degree perspective on deal management challenges and solutions.

Since 2013, Jill has dedicated herself exclusively to mastering the art and science of Deal Desks, working with some of the most innovative public companies and fastest-growing startups in the tech industry. Her unique blend of strategic vision and hands-on experience has helped numerous companies increase their deal velocity by up to 40 percent and boost average deal sizes by 33 percent or more.

Jill's approach is anything but one-size-fits-all. She's known for her ability to dive deep into a company's unique challenges, crafting bespoke solutions that align perfectly with each organization's unique goals and culture. From creating comprehensive playbooks to designing intricate approval matrices, Jill's strategies have become the secret weapon for businesses looking to scale without sacrificing compliance or profitability.

But Jill isn't just about the numbers. She's a passionate advocate for the transformative power of well-run Deal Desks, believing they're the unsung heroes of the startup world. Her energetic speaking style and ability to break down complex concepts into actionable insights have made her a sought-after speaker at industry conferences and a valued mentor to up-and-coming Deal Desk professionals.

When she's not revolutionizing deal processes, Jill embraces life's adventures—from coastal camping trips across California to yoga retreats on sun-soaked Mexican beaches to global travels that expand her perspective. At home, she channels her creativity into culinary experiments (yes, she's perfecting her sourdough game) and stays grounded through community service with local youth programs. Her boundless energy and authentic passion for both work and life inspire everyone around her to reach for excellence.

Jill is also the founder and president of Deal Solutions Consulting, LLC, a specialized consulting firm providing comprehensive Business and Deal Desk services to startups and established companies. Through Deal Solutions Consulting, Jill offers virtual Deal Desk support, complete Deal Desk buildouts, training programs, and ongoing optimization services, allowing businesses of all sizes to benefit from her extensive expertise.

With this book, Jill is on a mission to democratize Deal Desk knowledge, giving startups of all sizes the tools they need to compete with the big players. You'll learn proven, immediately actionable strategies to accelerate deal velocity, maximize deal values, and build the infrastructure needed for sustainable, profitable growth. Get inspired, challenged, and equipped to take your startup's deal game to the next level. Welcome to the Deal Desk revolution, led by the incomparable Jill Marie Roman.

A REQUEST FOR YOUR FEEDBACK

Thank You for Reading The Deal Desk Advantage!

Your insights are invaluable in helping me improve future editions and create resources that truly meet your needs. If you found this book helpful in your deal management journey, I'd be grateful if you could take a moment to share your experience.

Please consider leaving a brief review on Amazon.

Your feedback helps other leaders discover these strategies and encourages me to continue developing practical resources for the business community.

With much appreciation,

Jill